Gu

Pembrokeshire
Coast Path

with
Walking Times and Distances
of each section, plus short walks

by Tony Roberts

Sketch Maps and Illustrations
by Elizabeth Roberts

Abercastle Publications

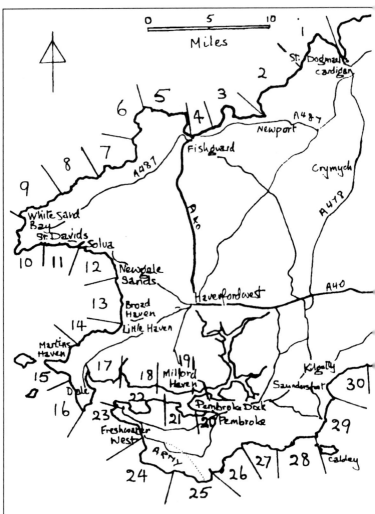

- The Coast Path has been divided into 30 sections, starting in the North. Many of these sections are further subdivided by time and distance. The detail thereby gained in terms of short walks makes this guide extremely useful for people wishing to explore small sections of the Coast Path, as well as allowing flexibility to those walking the whole path.
- The Contents page 3 gives the page number for each section.
- Distance and estimated time of walking shown at the head of each section.

Contents

Section | Page

	Introduction	4
1.	St Dogmael's to Ceibwr Bay	6
2.	Ceibwr Bay to Newport Sands	8
3.	Newport Sands to Aberbach (Hescwm)	12
	Note on the Antiquities of the area	15
4.	Aberbach (Hescwm) to Fishguard and Goodwick	16
5.	Harbour Village, Goodwick to Strumble Head	18
6.	Strumble Head to Penbwchdy	20
7.	Penbwchdy to Aberfelin (Trefin)	22
8.	Aberfelin (Trefin) to Aberpwll	24
9.	Aberpwll to Whitesands (St David's)	26
	The St David's Peninsula	28
	St David's, Cathedral and Close	29
10.	Whitesands to Caerfai	30
11.	Caerfai to Solva	33
12.	Solva to Newgale	35
13.	Newgale to Little Haven	36
14.	Little Haven to St Bride's	38
15.	St Bride's to Marloes Sands	39
16.	Marloes Sands to St Ann's Head	42
17.	St Ann's Head to Sandy Haven	42
18.	Sandy Haven to Milford	46
19.	Milford to Pembroke Dock	49
20.	Pembroke to Bentlass	50
21.	Bentlass to Texaco Car Park	53
22.	Texaco Car Park to West Angle Bay	54
23.	West Angle Bay to Freshwater West	56
24.	Freshwater West to Stack Rocks	57
25.	Stack Rocks to Broad Haven	60
26.	Broad Haven to Trewent Point	63
27.	Freshwater East to Manorbier	64
28.	Manorbier to Penally	66
29.	Giltar Point – Tenby – Monkstone Point	69
30.	Monkstone Point – Saundersfoot – Amroth	70
	Information on Public Transport	72

2006 edition.   Copyright © Tony Roberts.
Published by Abercastle Publications, Waunblaen, Felinwynt, Aberteifi, SA43 1RW.
This booklet was first published in 1973 and has been revised regularly.
Printed by Gwasg Dinefwr Press, Llandybïe

INTRODUCTION

Officially 170 miles long, the Coast Path may be over 200 miles taking into account the ups and downs that cannot be measured on a map. The naturalist R. M. Lockley surveyed a path in 1951; it was satutorily designated in 1952 and officially 'opened' in 1970.

The many intervening years were taken up by Local Authorities obtaining agreement with farmers and landowners for access over individual lengths of coast. Most gave it willingly; some were difficult; in a few cases, their fears have been justified: visitors do trespass, break down fences, tread down crops, leave gates open and let their dogs worry farm stock; but relatively very few.

All but 10% of the land round the coast is privately owned; and this applies to cliffs and beaches above the high water mark. Below, the beaches have been leased by the Crown to the County Council and there are By-Laws about behaviour, though they are never posted up anywhere.

The Coast Path runs from St Dogmael's to Amroth; most of the way it is on cliff-top, at times on the beach and at times on the road. Occasionally one has to go through towns and the Army prevents access at Castlemartin.

The stiles have now been numbered so that if you want to report something amiss to the National Park Authority, you can use the stile number as co-ordinate.

This Guide was the first guide to the Coast Path. It is reissued annually thereby enabling it to be constantly brought up to date. Whilst sections of the path are regularly walked for pleasure as well as research - the publisher would be grateful to receive any comments on the book for future improvements and up-dating.

A few points to note ...

● The distance given for each stretch is approximate, i.e. measured on a 6" map (and verified with a pedometer); the times are for a reasonably leisurely walk, but not allowing for stops. You will be lucky to average more than 2 miles an hour for most of the path (except for road parts). The maps are drawn to an approximate 2½" to the mile scale.

● Take care: the Coast Path is often dangerous. Someone is usually hurt every year; and there are few warnings. Much of the path is unsuitable for young children or elderly people.

● Wear strong shoes. A walking stick is also useful both for stability if the path is a bit slippery and to hold any straying brambles aside.

● Please don't take short cuts across

fields; keep off crops.

Footpaths are shown by dotted lines, and the Coast Path by a crossed line.

Geology

The county divides into North and South – in the North, Pre-Cambrian and Lower Palaeozoic rocks, folded and contorted in the great volcanic earth movements of Caledonian times 500 million years ago. In the south, newer, but still ancient rocks (Old Red Limestone and Carboniferous Limestone, with coal measures from St. Brides Bay to Saundersfoot) were subjected to Armorican folding 250 million years ago.

Erosion, both marine and glacial, has greatly affected the texture of the landscape; what has been left are two gently undulating surfaces, the so-called 600ft. and 200ft. platform.

Camping and Accommodation:

There is little accommodation right on the path. The best way is to use places as centres, and make day trips. Of course, it is possible to camp: remember, all the land, including the Coast Path, is private, so you should either find a recognised camp-site, or ask a farmer's permission to camp in his field. In addition there is the chain of Youth Hostels.

Note: Reference is made in the text to 'Fenton'. This is Richard Fenton, author of *A Historical Tour Through Pembrokeshire*, 1811.

St Dogmael's to Ceibwr Bay

Distance and Time: 7m. (first 3 on road); 2½ hrs. (1 road only).

Access and Condition of Path:

Go through St Dogmael's and on to Poppit Sands, turn left up the hill by the cafe. Another 1½m. of narrow road, pass YHA; finally a signpost takes you down, right, through a farmyard, out to the cliff. Car parking here and quarter mile earlier. Small charge. View over estuary to Cardigan Island, a Nature Reserve; gulls mainly, and a flock of rare Soay sheep.

The path is very good all the way. It is all on the cliff-top and mostly outside the fences. Be careful: though not difficult it is quite strenuous, so it is not really suitable for young children or the elderly.

Fp. from Pengarn Isaf to the old coastguard hut. Now a footpath from Pwll y Granant linking the coast path with the network of inland paths.

Description:

A very fine wild stretch of coast, after a laborious road start. Lonely; splendid high cliff scenery after low promontory of Cemaes Head. A rough, windswept landscape, with heather, bracken, gorse and rough grass. Mixed farming, mostly dairy, but some sheep and beef – so take care with dogs.

The rock strata are well displayed, especially the folding past Cemaes Head and at Pen-yr-afr. (Seen at its best walking northwards from Ceibwr). Pen-yr-afr

The 6th century Sagranus stone instrumental in the eventual decipherment of the Irish Ogam language.

and Ceibwr are National Trust (N.T) owned, the latter bequeathed by Wynford Vaughan-Thomas.

A splendid area for sea-birds – gulls galore including Great Black Backed, Choughs, Ravens, Fulmars, Kestrel, Buzzards; Stonechats everywhere, Jackdaws too. Choughs, so rare elsewhere in Britain, are relatively common on much of the Pembrokeshire coast; unmistakable, crows with red beak and legs.

Villages, Amenities and Short Walks:

St Dogmael's (W. Llandudoch), named after Celtic monk of 5th century whose cell was here. Sacked by Norse; 1113 Lord of Cemaes, Robert Martin, brought Reformed Benedictine monks and established an abbey, very grand in its day; now ruined. North transept north and west walls of nave still standing.

The monks are said to have introduced seine net fishing for salmon, still practised in the Teifi here. The village is pleasant and Victorian looking; church modern with some fascinating incised stone including Sagranus stone (6th C.- see drawing), important in deciphering the Ogam alphabet used by the Irish who colonised the area for several hundred years. Shops; pubs; PO, Y Felin flour mill.

Cafe/shop and Cardigan Lifeboat Station with shop staffed by volunteers at Poppit. Also phone, toilet and outside drinking water tap.

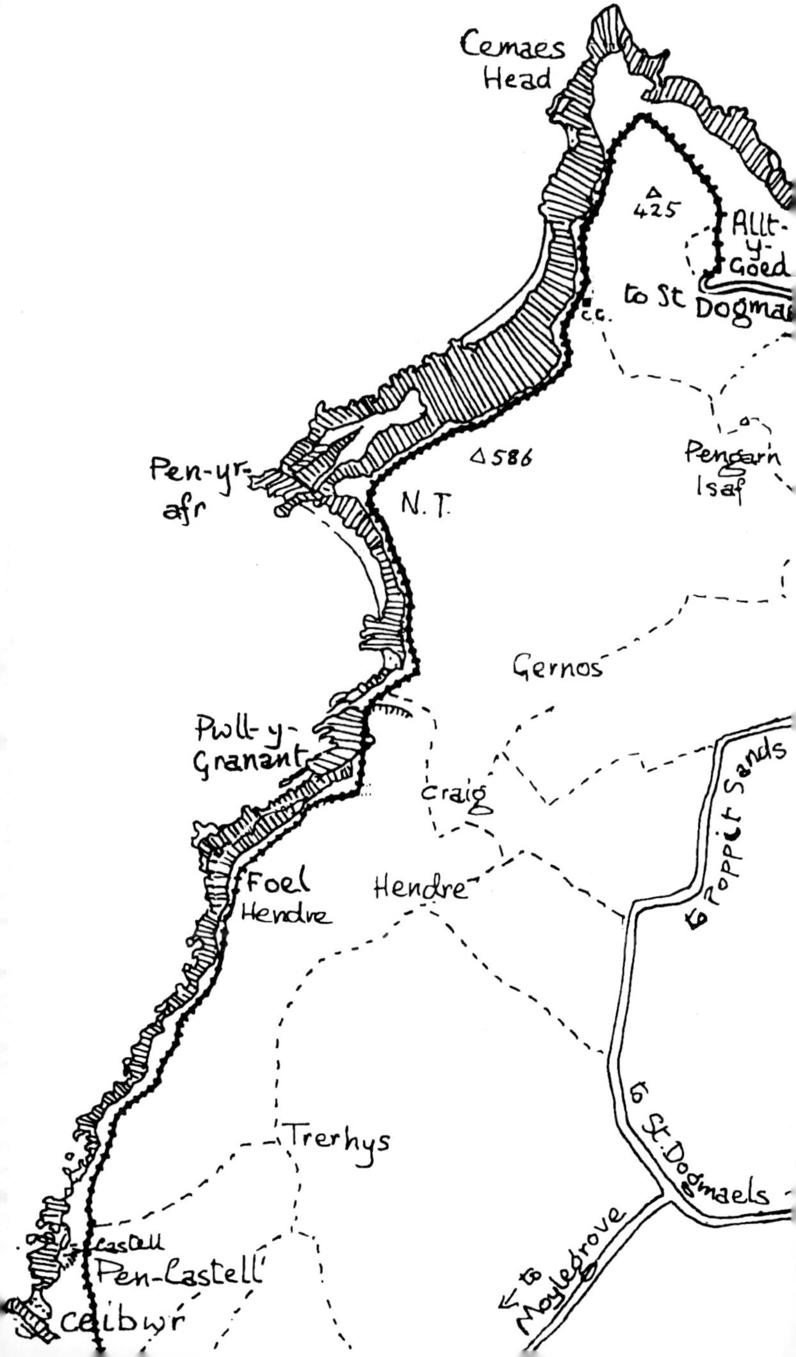

Cemaes Head

△ 425

Allt-y-Coed

to St Dogmael

△ 586

N.T.

Pengarn Isaf

Pen-yr-afr

Gernos

Poppit Sands

Pwll-y-Granant

Craig

Foel Hendre

Hendre

to St Dogmaels

Trerhys

Castell Pen-Castell

to Moylegrove

Ceibwr

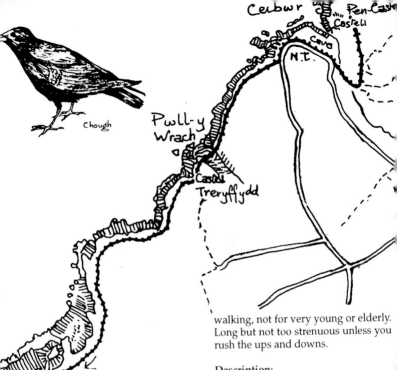

Chough

Ceibwr Bay to Newport Sands
Distance and time: 6m., 2¼ hours.

Access and Condition of Path:

Good car parking at both ends. National Park Car Park at Newport, road verges at Ceibwr. One intermediate access. Fp. at Pwll-y-Wrach ½ mile from Treriffith, but not good and parking very poor. County road runs ½ mile or more inland, parallel to coast, but no access before Newport Sands. A few hundred yards' walk on the road at Ceibwr at the start. Good, well-marked path, cliff-top all the way, mostly outside fence. Hard walking, not for very young or elderly. Long but not too strenuous unless you rush the ups and downs.

Description:

A splendid walk on a long, lonely and wild stretch, no buildings anywhere. Ceibwr is an attractive little bay, good for picnics but not for bathing, the beach is slightly scruffy with jetsam. Valley deepened here by glacial meltwater; cliffs show contorted strata produced by the great Caledonian earth movements, 450 million years ago. Ceibwr has good unofficial roadside parking, Seals to see, Gulls, Fulmars, Shags, Cormorants, Choughs on the grassy cliffs, Buzzards, Kestrels and Ravens.

Exquisite new Clapper bridge built by the National Park Authority at Ceibwr after the old bridge was washed away. The idea is that if the banks are washed away again this bridge can still be built out.

The cliffs along the coast are high

Llech-y-Drybedd

and craggy, fierce in winter, with jagged rocks, caves, arches, tiny, inaccessible shingly beaches and no people.

Pwll-y-Wrach (the Witches' Cauldron), half-a-mile from Ceibwr, is a collapsed cave; awe-inspiring in heavy weather. Castell Treriffith, immediately to the south of Pwll-y-Wrach, is an Iron Age hill fort, easy enough to spot when you know it is there, but otherwise confusing with a worn hedgebank; it forms a twin, so to speak, with the fort north of Ceibwr.

From Pwll-y-Wrach to Newport is one of the best solitary walks in the county. Cell Howel, after 1½m., is a long bracken-covered escarpment; then Foel Goch, a good place for seals, another mile; then Godir Tudor, a high sheer and inaccessible cleft where sea-birds nest, a mile more; Morfa Head is

½m., and Pen Pistill a small steep sided glen ½m. more, then Newport Sands.

Apart from the wild life – sea birds, seals, perhaps a fox or two, there are several notable prehistoric burial chambers within striking distance. The celebrated Pentre Ifan, in the foothills of the Preselies behind Newport, is not far and is too interesting to omit. Carreg Coetan Arthur is in Newport itself; and there are two others a little inland from here. Llech-y-Drybedd (Tripod Stone) (SN101432), is 1½m. from Moylegrove, left, off the road to Newport. Trellyffaint (SN 082425), a couple of fields in from the Newport-Moylegrove road 2½ miles north of Newport Sands. This chambered tomb has 35 Cupmarks engraved on it but the meaning of them is not known. For a little more of local archaeological interest see page 15.

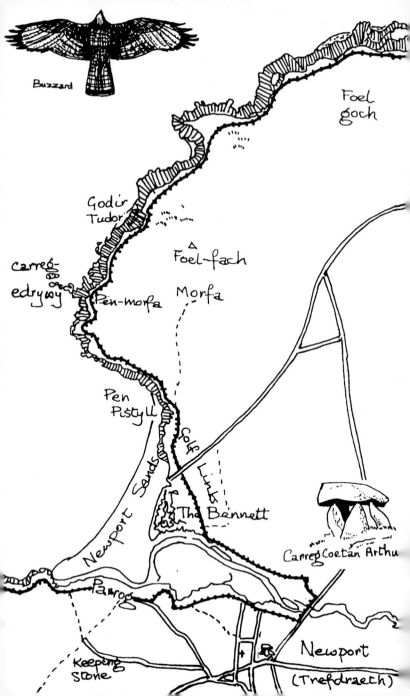

Buzzard

Foel goch

Godir Tudor

carreg-edrywy

Pen-morfa

Foel-fach

Morfa

Pen Pistyll

Newport Sands

Golf Links

The Bennett

Carreg Coetan Arthu

Parrog

Newport

(Trefdraeth)

Keeping Stone

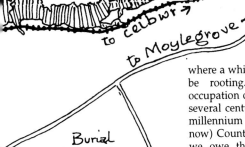

to Ceibwr →

to Moylegrove →

Burial
Chamber +

Villages, Amenities and Short Walks:

Moylegrove (W. Trewyddel), ½m. from Ceibwr Bay, Mathilda's Grove, from the wife of the original Marcher Lord. It is a small village which comes to life when the holiday homes are opened up – people from away can pay more for cottages and small-holdings than needy young locals. Toilets and phone in village.

Nevern (W. Nanhyfer), a short walk from the Coast Path and well worth the trouble, is a beautiful little village on a good salmon river. Narrow bridge, celebrated pub, but no shops. Church, late Perpendicular, interior restored. Like half-a-dozen others, the church is dedicated to St Brynach, a 5th century Irish-man, who after communing with the angels on Carn Ingli, was directed to build his church where a white sow with piglets would be rooting. There was an Irish occupation of much of West Wales for several centuries (3rd and 4th) of this millennium by the Deisi from (what is now) County Waterford, and to them we owe the Ogham inscriptions, a couple of which are to be found on commemorative stones in Nevern Church (and yard).

The church is also well worth a visit for its remarkably fine yew trees; the second from the right called 'the bleeding yew' from the sticky brown-red liquid that oozes from the trunk. Legend says this will bleed until a Welshman is again Lord of the Castle on the hill. There is also a splendid Celtic High Cross (Tenth Century) and cemented into a windowsill a beautiful, interlaced inscribed cross stone shown below.

Up the hill, 100 yards away, a rough cross is cut out of the rock, the last rest, according to tradition, of pilgrims from Strata Florida to St. David's. Nevern Castle, further up the hill, is largely earthwork remains.

Toilets, and ice-cream shop at Newport Sands.

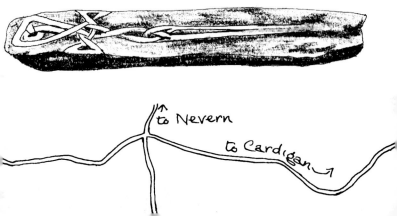

to Nevern

to Cardigan →

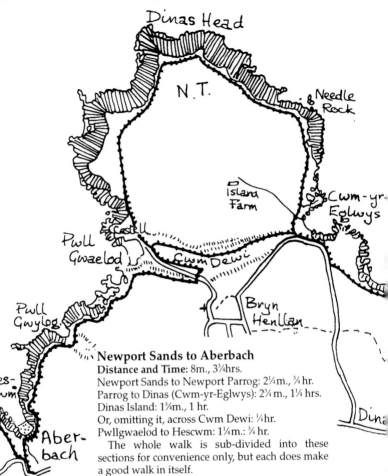

Dinas Head

N.T.

Needle Rock

Island Farm

Cwm-yr-Eglwys

Pwll Gwaelod

Castell

Cwm Dewi

Pwll Gwylog

Bryn Henllan

tes-wm

Dinas

Aberbach

Newport Sands to Aberbach

Distance and Time: 8m., 3¾hrs.
Newport Sands to Newport Parrog: 2¼m., ¾ hr.
Parrog to Dinas (Cwm-yr-Eglwys): 2¾ m., 1¼ hrs.
Dinas Island: 1¾m., 1 hr.
Or, omitting it, across Cwm Dewi: ¼hr.
Pwllgwaelod to Hescwm: 1¼m.: ¾ hr.

The whole walk is sub-divided into these sections for convenience only, but each does make a good walk in itself.

Access and Condition of Path:

Road access and good parking at Newport Sands, Parrog, Cwm-yr Eglwys, Pwllgwaelod. Access only at Aberbach. Private road access at Aberfforest.

Fp. access ¾m. further Newport and ¼m. further, at Aberrhigian, and ½m. more at Aberfforest.

Path is good everywhere, sometimes a bit overgrown in summer, but bear with it and don't go over into neighbouring cornfields; unless it well walked, there will be no path. Finding the path: go right across Newport Sands, then left up the estuary to the bridge, cross, turn right, skirting village. Well signposted. The path along the estuary from the iron bridge to the Parrog has been gravelled making it easy for pushchairs or with more difficulty possible for wheelchair users.

At Cwm-yr-Eglwys, path emerges on road; turn right, down hill to car park: the path is signposted either

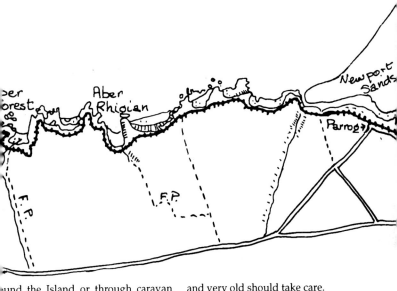

ound the Island or through caravan
ark across Cwm Dewi to Pwll-
waelod. The path through Cwm
ewi has been concreted to be
ccessable for wheelchair users.

escription:
Excellent coast and cliff scenery.
uite lonely in places despite the
any access points and proximity to
llages which make this one of the
andiest stretches in the County.
ood, easy walking, despite some
radients, all right for 10-year-olds,
ut, as everywhere else, the very young

and very old should take care.

Cliffs most of the way, low (100ft.-
200ft.), but sheer, descending to coves
and good swimming beaches at
Newport, Aberrhigian, Aberfforest,
Cwm-yr-Eglwys, Pwllgwaelod,
Aberbach. Typical windswept cliff
cover, gorse, bracken, bramble, few
trees, except in a cwm and then blackthorn, hazel, hawthorn, a little scrub-
oak and ash. Round the farms, the
trees are mostly ubiquitous sycamore,
hardiest of trees.

A pleasant walk round Newport to
start with, then low cliffs to Dinas,

13

Newport, with Iron Age fort Carn Ingli on top.

broken by cwms at Aberrhigian and Aberfforest. Cwm-yr-Eglwys has rather a swish air of an English sailing village, Pwllgwaelod more popular, grey sand, Restaurant/Cafe on beach. Aberbach is relatively deserted because of limited parking.

The A487 runs parallel to the coast, half a mile inland, and you see the outermost Preseli foothills on the skyline: Mynydd Melin, and Mynydd Llanllawer terminating in a rocky nipple, and, says Fenton, 'not inapppropriately called the Maiden's Breast from no other similitude to that lovely hemisphere but its roundness'.

Dinas Island can be omitted by going through Cwm Dewi, but it ought not to be, you really should walk round. Splendid views, and sea-birds even in the off-season; Herring, Great and Lesser Black Backed Gulls, Fulmars with their wheeling, sweeping, glide, and nesting in crevices, Shags, Cormorants, with thin white throat patch, Guillemots and Razorbills (the National Park symbol), huge jet Ravens, usually in pairs, looking less sinister here than on upland fields at lambing time, Choughs, Carrion Crows, Jackdaws, Feral (wild) Pigeons, Kestrel,

Buzzards. Away from the cliffs, Stone chats, Warblers.

Whether you see the carpeting o thyme, ling and bell-heather depend on the season – so too, the squills vetches, scabious, campions, orchids stone-crop, pennyworts, thrifts, fox gloves, the list is endless.

Two fine Burial Chambers are Car reg Coetan Arthur, already mentione in the last walk. Secondly, Cerrig Gof (Blacksmith's Stones), a uniqu group of five collapsed cromlechs in field by the A487 (a mile pas Newport) just past the footpath t Aberrhigian but do not expect th footpath to be signposted.

Villages, Amenities and Short Walks

Newport (Trefdraeth), a pleasan historic little village, still nominall the Seat of the Lords Marcher o Cemaes. Founded in 1195 by Willian de Turribus when he was ejected fron Nevern by the Welsh and built Newpo Castle. He also founded the Church, 121! The Castle is private. Fine gatewa and flanking tower. Some restora tion, then some public access w are told. A very good Norman fon

the church (restored 1854). In
zabethan times, woollen manu-
'turing and a thriving port, espe-
lly with Bristol. The sand-bar, men-
ned by George Owen, 1603, is still
:re. Some very pleasant early cot-
;es and houses, and good typical
apels. But lots of modern houses,
ne nice some ill-suited. Big English
lux, here and Dinas. Shops, restau-
ts, P.O., pubs, garages, art galleries.
·od book-shop. Information Centre.
:o   West-Wales   Eco-centre   -
ormation on environmental issues
d energy saving. Resourse centre
th leaflets, magazines and books.
Dinas, pop. 500, is a long strag-
ng village mainly on the A40, but
th the two beaches, Cwm-yr-
lwys and Pwllgwaelod, at either
d of the valley joining Dinas island
the mainland. Toilets at both.
vm-yr-Eglwys was Dinas Harbour;
e great storm of 1859 wrecked St

Brynach's Church on the shore.
Shops and cafés, garages and Post
Office at Dinas.

Short walks are very good, either
inland or on the Coast Path. The
footpaths can be used to break up the
Coast Path into shorter walks: Parrog
to Aberrhigian, for example, is 1¼m.,
Aberrhigian to Aberfforest ¾m.

ote on the Antiquities of the area

North   Pembrokeshire,   has   an
rivalled accumulation of prehistoric
es. A few have been noted in passing
eady, and if you can find a copy of
e first official National Park Guide
MSO 1973, ed. Dilwyn Miles) read
e fascinating and ample section on
chaeology by Professor W. F. Grimes.
e Nevern Valley and its environs is
pecially good for Neolithic mega-
hic monuments, some of which have

already been mentioned; Bronze Age
standing stones, very
few of which have been
excavated and which
may be part of more
extensive, and as yet
unknown, ritual sites;
and, finally, Iron Age
coastal promontory forts
and inland fortified
settlements.   One   of
these, Castell Henllys, is being excavated and is open to the public; well
worth a visit (just past Felindre
Farchog on the A487 on the way to
Cardigan).

Pembrokeshire has long been a
Mecca for geologists; it is also one of
the most interesting areas in Britain for
archaeologists   and   students   of
mythology and folklore (see also our
Myths and Legends of Pembrokeshire).

Aberbach (Hescwm) to Fishguard & Goodwick

Distance and Time: 5m., 2hrs.
Hescwm to the Old Fort,
Fishguard: 2½m., 1¼hrs.
Old Fort to Harbour Village,
Goodwick: 2½m., ¾hr.

Access and Condition of Path:

Fp. at Hescwm, walk through Hescwm Mill to the beach or start on the hill a few yards west. Plenty of parking space at the Old Fort, Fishguard, and a car park at Goodwick end.

Condition of the path is good all the way. Easy walking; a few slopes but nothing difficult. Through Fishguard and Goodwick you go on the road but there is a pleasant marine walk round Fishguard.

Description:

Hescwm to Fishguard is excellent walking, quite solitary apart from going through caravan site. Striking cliff scenery west of Penrhyn – the path is on the cliff-top all the way getting rougher with more rock and heather nearer Fishguard. The same kind of sea-bird colonies as on the previous stretch though not in such profusion as at Dinas Island.

The Old Fort, where you reach Fishguard, was, unlike the Milford Haven fortifications, a late 18th century construction, after a privateer had scared Fishguard by an all-day bombardment.

Over the hills to the south is Cwm Gwaun, an unspoilt, steeply wooded valley of small farms, celebrated for home-brewed beer and keeping the Old pre-Gregorian New Year, January 13th. Good walking on narrow roads and numerous fps. Also Dinas and Newport Mountains – with heather and gorse, sheep and wild ponies.

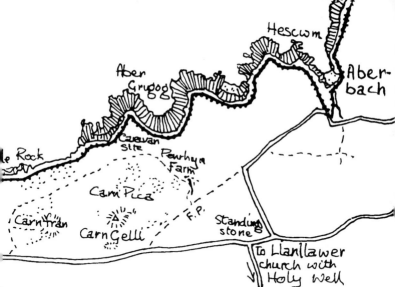

Villages, Amenities and Short walks:
Fishguard, (Market Thursday), is in two parts: firstly, Lower Town (Y Cwm) is the original Abergwaun (mouth of the river Gwaun) and then Fishguard itself, up the hill and then descending via the Parrog where Goodwick joins it.

Lower Town, reminiscent of an unspoilt Provencal village, is charming, with a good tidal harbour and lots of small boats. There is a narrow bridge over the Gwaun, rebuilt C. on the west side of which is a footpath.

Fishguard was the leading port on the north coast until the railways came. In the 19th century, about 50 coasting vessels came here. Paradoxically, communications were better on the Pembroke-shire coast before the railway era. Coal and lime were brought in from everywhere by sea

and grain and dairy produce taken out.

Old stone cottages mingle with new development. Some good chapel architecture, especially Hermon with its classical façade.

Goodwick, across the moor, is a 'railway' town with a late Victorian look. The harbour was built in 1906; millions of tons of rock were blasted away. The trans-Atlantic liners came and went; even the cattle trade from Ireland has now ceased.

Fishguard is now a ferry port for Ireland and a focal point for the enormous container trucks which clog up the roads and damage the country bridges, but nobody can manage to work out an acceptable by-pass.

Very good walks. C.P. either way has good access; also up the Gwaun valley and the hills north and south.

Harbour Village, Goodwick, to Strumble Head
Distance and Time: 6m., 2¾ hrs.

Access and Condition of Path:
Car park at either end; Fp. at Carreg Wastad from Trehowel Farm and from Llanwnda; Fp. at Penrhyn and to Porthsychan from Tresinwen (limited space for cars). Much of this path is hard and rough; not for young children; and not in shorts. Sometimes the path is hard to trace.

Description:
A good, long, lonely stretch of excellent walking. Different from the previous coast; this is the bare Pencaer peninsula; local volcanic activity produced the worn rocky prominences behind the coastal area from Garnwnda to Garn Fawr. Exposed small farms, absentee holiday cottagers and remoteness. An unpromising start at Harbour Village, though, past derelict allotments, tin cans, brambles, plastic and the charred and rotting stumps of what Lockley described as a pine wood. The uninitiated will have very great difficulty in finding the burial chambers at Penrhiw and Garn Wen.

The path leads quickly to a clear stony landscape, heather, bracken in places and coarse grass. As you round Carn Fathach, the view of Llanwnda, with Ciliau moor and Garn-wnda behind, makes as fine a picture inland as the tongues of headland one after another on the seaward side. The going is rough either side of Carreg Wastad where a stone pillar commemorates the abortive French invasion of 1797. In this bizarre episode, 1,400 men, half soldiers, half from the jails under an elderly American called Tate, landed with the intention of marching to Liverpool and burning it, pillaging and looting as they went. But they got drunk, looted the farms of Pencaer, and Tate surrendered, without fighting, on Goodwick sands two days later to the local yeomanry.

A mile west of Carreg Wastad brings you to Penrhyn (fp. to road), tiny holiday cottage, and a half a mile more to Porth Sychan (Fp. to road) an attractive little bay. You pass the site of St Degan's chapel but there are no remains of it visible. The other site is Porth Sychan is Carreg Gibi, named after Cornish Saint Cybi, another of the early Celtic saints who sailed so widely round the wild coasts. There is a fine St. Cybi's well on the Llyn peninsular and Caergybi is the Welsh for Holyhead.

18

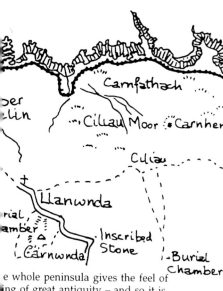

e whole peninsula gives the feel of
ing of great antiquity – and so it is.

Goodwick are Carn Wen
(M947390) and Penrhiw (SM943391)
omlechs. The cromlech above
anwnda is Carn Wnda (SM933392)
ub-megalithic' –which is achieved
putting one end of the capstone on
e ground and the other on a
pporter in a pit). Gyllwch, at the
ot of Garn Gilfach (SM908390) has a
pstone with four supporters; and 30
rds to the south are the remains of
other cromlech.

Villages & Amenities

Llanwnda, is really only a collection
of houses, no shop, café, or Post
Office. The parish church, rebuilt 1881,
is a simple Celtic one, with several
incised stones, well worth looking at,
set in exterior walls.

Short Walks: The footpaths can be
used to break up the C. P. and are
good rough walking. The roads, too,
round Pencaer peninsula are good
walking in themselves.

Strumble Head to Pen Bwchdy

Distance and Time: 4 m. to Pen Bwchdy; 5 to Pwllcrochan; 2 hrs. and 2½ respectively.

Access and Condition of Path:

Car parking at Strumble Head and at Pwllderi in the middle of the stretch; no access at all at Pen Bwchdy, where the map finishes, but Fp. at Pwllcrochan 1 mile further on. There is a short walk on the road at Strumble Head and at Pwllderi too. The path is not too well defined about Pwll Arian, by Pen Brush and Pen Bwchdy, but persevere, you cannot go wrong. It can be quite rough going and it is not for young children.

Description:

A superb stretch of rough walking. Remote and wild, a rocky waste with bracken, heather, coarse grass. Precipitous cliffs, shared with Gulls, Ravens, Choughs, possibly a Peregrine. Grey seals at Pwllderi.

Strumble Head Lighthouse, built 1908, on the island Ynys Michael, connected by a bridge. Has good car park, but is now automatic.

At Pwllderi is a youth hostel, in a most magnificent position. On the road nearby is a memorial to Dewi Emrys, the poet. Behind Pwllderi towers, Garn Fawr, one of the finest stone forts in Britain, despite depredations for wall-building. Several lines of stone ramparts connect the rock outcrops and there is an earth rampart and ditch; best approached from the car park on the landward side.

Dinas Mawr, half mile west of Garn Fawr, is a fine promontory cliff fort; three sides are steep precipices to the sea; the narrow neck connecting it to landward is fortified by two stone banks.

South of Pwllderi is Trefasser, hamlet and farm, said to be the birthplace of Bishop Asser, 707 A.D., friend and biographer of Alfred the Great.

Villages, Amenities and Short Walks:

No amenities. Footpaths all rather limited so the best walks are on the Coast Path, starting from Strumble Head and Pwllderi — equally fine in all directions.

Other *Abercastle Publications*

Porthgain
St. Davids
Geology of Pembrokeshire
Best Walks in Pembrokeshire
Myths and Legends of Pembrokeshire
Myths and Legends of Wales
Welsh Herbal Medicine
Coastal Gardening

Available in a wide range of outlets – Bookshops, Information Centres, Newsagents, Craft Shops . . .

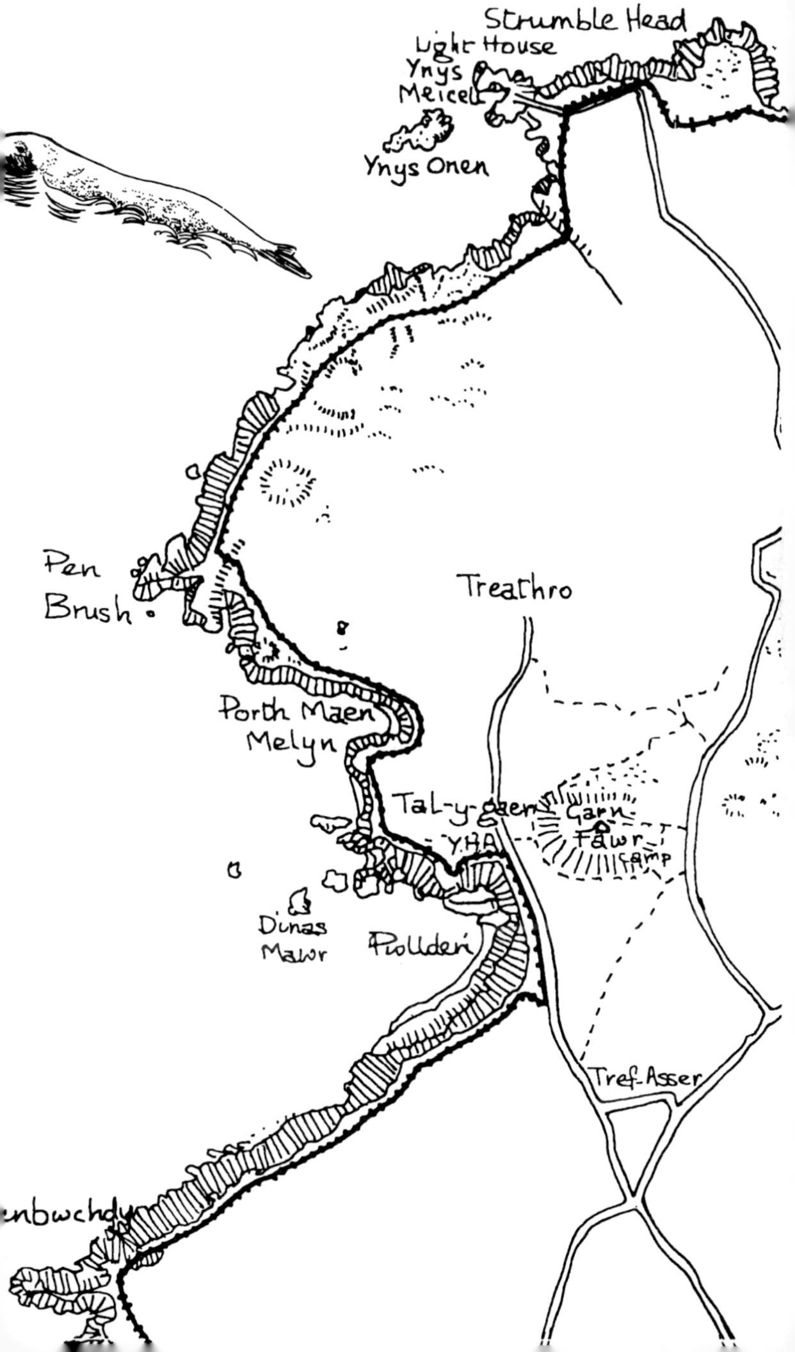

Strumble Head

Light House

Ynys Meicell

Ynys Onen

Pen Brush .

Treathro

Porth Maen Melyn

Tal-y-gaen
YHA

Garn Fawr
Camp

Dinas Mawr

Piollderi

Tref-Asser

nbwchdy

Pen Bwchdy to Aberfelin (Trefin)

Distance and Time: 8¼m., 4½hrs.
Pen Bwchdy to Abermawr: 2¼m., 1¼hrs.
Pwllcrochan to Abermawr: 1¼m., ½hr.
Abermawr to Abercastle: 2¼m., 1¼hrs.
Abercastle to Aberfelin: 2½m., 1½hrs.

Access and Condition of the Path:

Car parking on the verges at Abermawr and Aberbach. Limited parking too, at Abercastle and Aberfelin. Fp. from Velindre Farm to Pwllcrochan. Fp. at Aberbach, where the coast path is signposted on the road for 100 yds. but a path goes round the headland. Fp. too from road (believe it or not, a county road, but do not try to take a car down it) by Carnachenllwyd Farm to Pwllstrodyr and Fp. again from the road to the coast via Longhouse Cromlech; Fp. from Trefin to coast.

The path is good and walkable all the way to Aberbach. It is roughish at times but for the most part, the going is easy. Very narrow and quite dangerous at times with sheer cliffs by Longhouse; take great care with children.

Description:

North of Aberbach, the walk is really a continuation of the rough exhilarating one down from Strumble Head. Quiet, lonely, unspoilt, supe coast and cliff scenery. Past Abermaw is Mynydd Morfa, a rough headlam an indented coastline with fi beaches, but inaccessible. Fro thereabouts to Aberfelin, the farmlam is better, but all this area has fine ear potato fields. Much of the walking outside the fence. The Coast Path h been knocked about a bit at Abermaw

The lonely rocky coast above Abe mawr, is one of the best places to s seals, especially in the autumn breeding time (when they should o no account be disturbed). There a sea-bird colonies, fine ones Guillemots, and Razorbills south Pwllcrochan.

Tregwynt Mill is a working woolle mill, one of the remaining few in t County, open to visitors. Shop and cafe

At Abermawr the small white buildir was at one time the trans-Atlan submarine cable terminus.

Good swimming beaches at Pw crochan, Aberbach, Abermawr, Abe castle and Aberfelin. Most beaches a rocky with pebbles at high water ar sand at low.

There is a fine cromlech, Ffyst Samso at Trellys, south of St Nicholas; also the Parish is Ffynnon Drudic cromlech, 3m. inland towards Goodwic

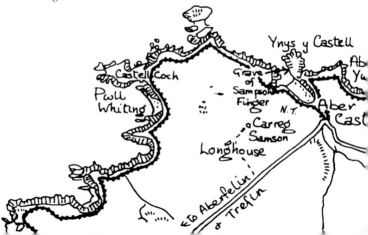

n the farm of that name. At Longhouse, Carreg
amson (about 3000 B.C.) is one of the most famous
romlechs of all (Fp. access and car parking). Another
romlech, ruined, is at Trewallter Llwyd, west of Mathry.

Promontory forts at Pen Morfa, Ynys-y-Castell; at
Abercastle and Pencastell Coch, past Abercastle where
he cliffs are fine and sheer.

Part of the coast path and areas inland at Abercastle
nd Abermawr are now owned and managed by the N. T.

Very low tides at Abermawr, as at Whitesands,
reshwater West and Amroth, show the tree stumps of
he submerged coastal forests, drowned on the melting
f the last Ice Age.

Villages Amenities and Short Walks:

Abercastle: Once a small port, its ships trading with
Bristol and Liverpool. Nothing but a beach now and
cottages. Toilets. Limited parking for short walks either
way. Fine lime kiln to south of harbour and ruined
granary to the north beside the Coast Path – but try and
prevent children playing about in it, it is private
anyway and the structure is said to be dangerous.

Trefin: Large village, shop, pub, YHA, craft centre.

Fps. lead to the coast at distances which allow good
hort walks: for example, Aberbach to Pwllcrochan, or
Abermawr to Abercastle; Abercastle to Trefin.

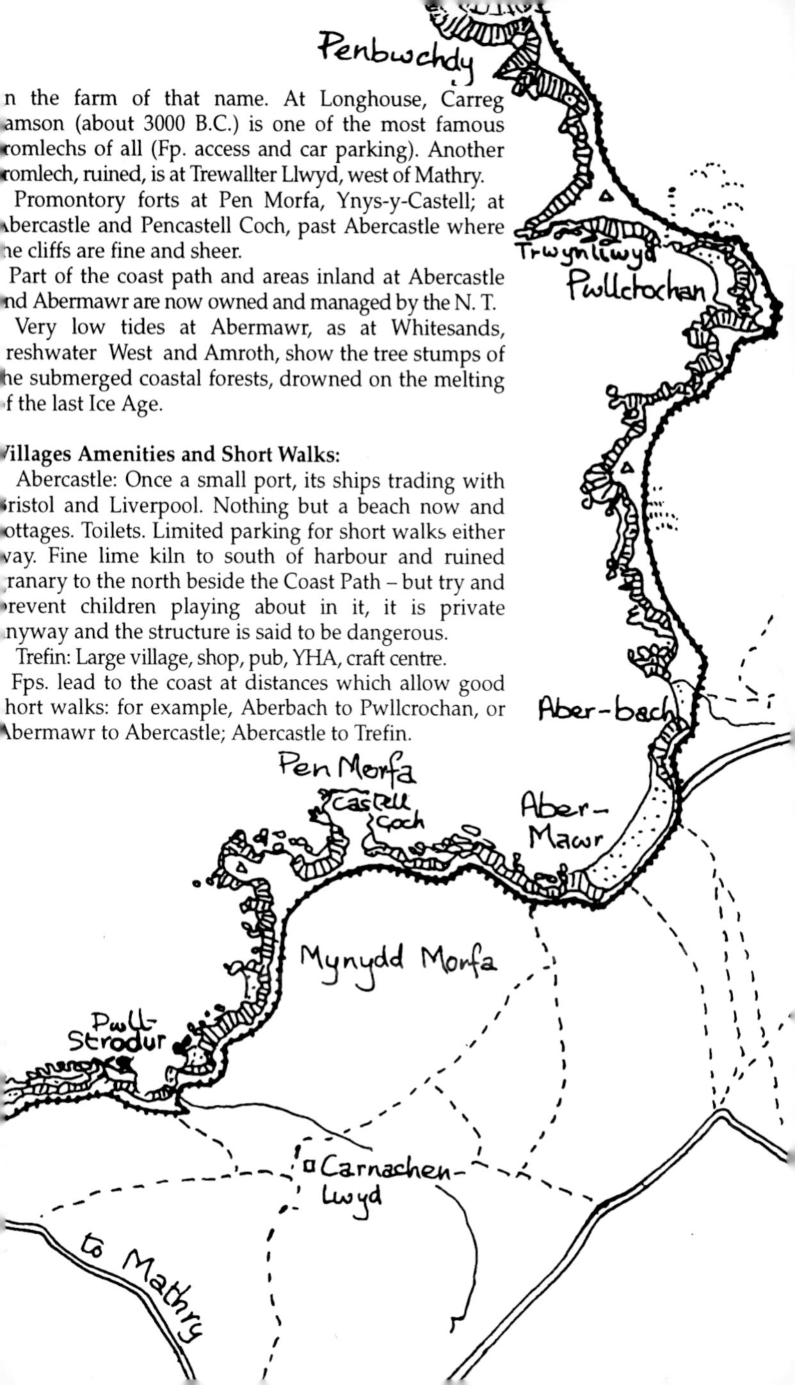

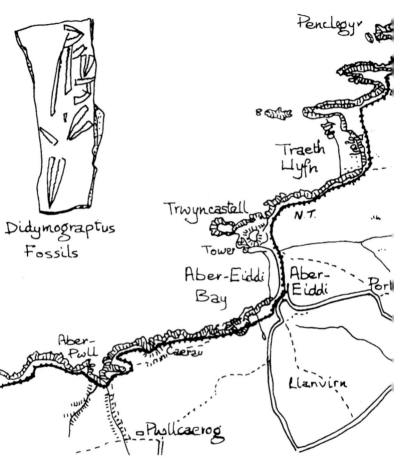

Didymograptus
Fossils

Penclegyr

Traeth
Llyfn

Trwyncastell   N.T.

Tower

Aber-Eiddi
Bay

Aber-
Eiddi

Por

Aber-
Pwll

Tyddyn Caerau

Pwllcaerog

Llanvirn

Aberfelin to Aberpwll

Distance and Time: 4¾ m., 2¼ hrs.
Aberfelin to Porthgain: 2 m., ¾ hr.
Porthgain to Abereiddi: 1½ m., ¾ hr.
Abereiddi to Aberpwll: 1¼ m., ¾ hr.

Access and Condition of Path:

Car parking at Aberfelin, Porthgain
and Abereiddi, and, though not
official, there is plenty of room usually
at the latter two. Cars may possibly
also be left near Pwllcaerog Farm, for

the Fp. access Pwllcaerog to Aberpwl
Inland Fp. from Pwllcaerog t
Llanvirn. All quite easy walking wit
a good path, except for the rutted bi
from Porthgain to Trathllyfn.

Description:

A delightful area for coast walking
Also popular for holiday cottages – th
'remote' and 'unknown to tourist
guide-book adjectives of ten years ag
no longer apply. It is not yet over

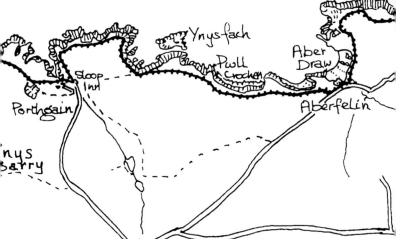

rowded but it has not the solitude of the Pencaer peninsula, though the villages and pubs are better.

A fairly gentle walk past bays and headland to Porthgain, then again to Abereiddi, passing Traethllyfn, a splendid beach.

Sea-birds and wild flowers, very fine.

There is an Iron Age fort just before Aberpwll, off the coast.

Abereiddi, or more properly, Llanirn, a farm close by, is the type locality of this division of Ordovician rocks, with plentiful fossil 'tuning fork' graptolites to be found on the beach or at least they used to be plentiful. The coastline between Porthgain and Abereiddi is all now National Trust. There are ongoing plans to preserve the industrial ruins.

Villages, Amenities and Short Walks:

Porthgain formerly had fishing and quarrying. The small harbour (improved in 1902) exported crushed stone up to 1931. Despite a derelict air, the place is very alive, with a pub, art gallery and a restaurant. Toilets. But the stone workings are defunct and the crushers and bins empty. The shell of a building in the harbour has been restored, but the whole place could be spoiled by any but the most careful development. In the Spring of 1981, the houses were sold to local people and the National Park Authority bought the ruins and harbour. Pub is celebrated. There is a booklet 'About Porthgain' on the history of this unusual industrial area in this series.

Llanrhian is a hamlet ½-mile inland from Porthgain. Small, attractive church. The Manor house, farm buildings and Trevacoon, on the road to St David's, are interesting buildings.

Croesgoch, a crossroads village, is on the A487, up the road from Llanrhian. Shop and Post Office, pub and handsome Baptist chapel, art gallery.

Abereiddi: by the shore, splendid old cottages and a few ill-fitting modern ones. Toilets. A dark slaty bay, strangely attractive; to the north, the Blue Lagoon, man-made, still and deep. Slates were exported from here by tramway to the harbour at Porthgain. Unable to compete with Caernarvon slate, it closed in 1904.

The numerous roads and footpaths shown on the map provide a veritable network of walks, coastal and inland. The going is never hard.

Aberpwll to Whitesands (St David's)

Time and Distance: 5¾m., 2¾hrs.
Aberpwll to Penbiri: 1¼m., ¾hr.
Penbiri to Whitesand: 4m., 2hrs.

Access and Condition of Path:

Car parking not easy along this stretch: on road, verge probably. Large car park at Whitesand, small charge. Fp. access via farms as on sketch-map dotted line. Condition of access paths should be O.K.; Coast Path clear and good all the way.

withstood the erosion that has worn down the older rocks inland and to the south and they were islands when the sea was 200 feet higher.

The seabirds are splendid here, and you may be lucky and see a Peregrine. A tremendous profusion of wild flowers throughout spring and summer. But around Carn Llidi and St David's Head, it is the evidence of prehistoric man that makes so deep an impression. The small fields of the Iron Age Celts can be seen clearly when the bracken isn't high, to the landward side of Carn Llidi.

St David's Head (Penmaen Dewi)

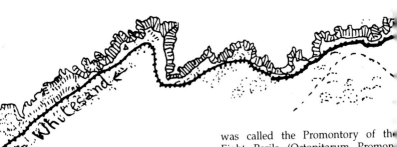

Description:

A majestic and superbly impressive stretch of coast. Carn Llidi – St David's Head area – is popular in summer. Aberpwll-Penbiri is a little less so. It is wild and craggy on the seaward side of the hills, with the landward side well farmed until you come to Carn Llidi which is a heathery waste, as it was in Fenton's day. Cliff-top walk all the way, no access to beach except at Porth Melgan near the end. On the outside of fences most of the way, wonderful views. The hills look huge and impressive, but so flat is the landscape that this is an illusion: they are under 600 feet. These peaks of Ordovician volcanic rock have

was called the Promontory of the Eight Perils (Octopitarum Promontarium) by the geographer Ptolemy for off here are some of the deadliest rocks to early shipping, the Bishop and Clerks. Inland, ½-mile to the east is a cromlech, Coetan Arthur, the capstone now resting on only one supporter; up beneath Carn Llidi are two more burial chambers, sub-megalithic this time. Most fascinating is the promontory fort on St David's Head to which an ancient trackway leads. There is a great stone barrier across the Head, Clawdd-y-Milwyr (The Warriors' Dyke) and inside eight stone hut circles.

Whitesand Bay (Porth Mawr) is one of the finest stretches of sand in West Wales, superb both for bathing and

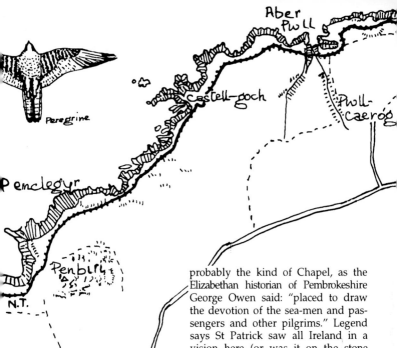

Peregrine

Castell-goch

Aber Pwll

Pwll-caerog

Pemclegyr

Penbiri

N.T.

probably the kind of Chapel, as the Elizabethan historian of Pembrokeshire George Owen said: "placed to draw the devotion of the sea-men and passengers and other pilgrims." Legend says St Patrick saw all Ireland in a vision here (or was it on the stone bench, at the Treasurer's House?) and resolved to return to convert the Irish.

...rfing. A submerged forest has been revealed at low water, as at Newgale and Amroth.

There is so much to see and experience covering memories – and folk memories – over a couple of thousand years.

The megalithic people were here; the Bronze Age too; and later the Iron Age people – the last have even left the outlines of their small arable fields on the landward side of Carn Llidi.

The associations with early Christianity abound: St Patrick's Chapel, Ty Gwyn, St Nons, St Davids well, St Justinian's, Clegyr Boia, you feel it every time you walk here.

Just north of the car park is the site of St Patrick's Chapel. The building was now completely gone but it was 30ft. by 13ft. internally and was

Villages, Amenities and Short Walks:

St David's is a fine centre for walking or touring. Good hotel accommodation. Information Centre, cafes, N.T. shop, a good bookshop to browse in and, of course, the Cathedral and Bishop's Palace to visit. Some of the best self-catering cottages in Britain round here.

No villages, apart from St David's, two miles away, but shop, toilets, telephone at the car park at Whitesand. Nearby are a Youth Hostel, camping and a Hotel.

St. David's Head is now owned by the National Trust. The heathery waste allows you to wander pretty much at will, but there is in fact an abundance of footpaths around Carn Llidi and linking with Coast path.

Map labels: N.T. — Carnec Lleith — Carnllidi — Burial Chambers — Coetan arthur (Cromlech) — Enclosures — Hut Circles — Crisal — (camp) — Porth Melgan — St Davids Head — Maen Sigl — Pwll Uog — St Patricks Chapel — car park — Whitesand Bay or Porth-Mawr — Traeth-mawr — The Burrows or Tywyn — Llaethdy Y.H.A. — Trefelly — St Da

The St David's Peninsula

The early spread of Christianity in Britain centred to a large extent on this rugged coast, an intersection of the sea-route from N.W. Europe to N.W. England and Ireland, and the land route eastwards across England and Wales.

The 'Peregrini' (travelling Celtic Saints) made their long missionary journeys and set up tiny beehive cells (Llan – a holy place) after landing on these rocky shores. When Saint David established his cell, and later removed his see from Caerleon to St David's, the wild and desolate peninsula became a place of pilgrimage equal to Compostela in N.W. Spain, and second to Rome.

But 1,000 years before this, the Preseli Hills held a deep religious significance for the Bronze Age peoples; and the ancient track-way over the hills led to Whitesand and the trade route for Irish gold and copper.

Even earlier, 1,000 years further back, the Megalith builders of the Neolithic Age used the same sea-route. Until the coming of the railways, sea journeying in these dangerous waters was the normal method of travel. But the railway never came to St David's. So the peninsula remained isolated until the coming of motor-cars.

St David's, Cathedral and Close

A stimulating place for anyone with some historical imagination. The city a prelude to the Cathedral; architecturally insignificant with buildings from Vernacular Grot to Bungaloid Modern; and a modernistic monstrosity of an Information Centre.

But the Cathedral, ruined Bishop's Palace and Close are a fine medieval grouping in a more rural ecclesiastical setting than any in Britain, and as handsome as any. True, the houses in the Close are later than medieval, but the weathered stone is admirable. Well worth a day's deviation from the Coast Path.

From the city, you can't see the Cathedral and Close built in the little valley perhaps to shelter from the wind and later, perhaps, from predatory Vikings.

St David founded his cell and austere order in mid-6th century. But what we see dates from five hundred or more years later when the Norman, de Leia, built a large cathedral in late 12th century. The tower collapsed, as many Norman towers did, and was rebuilt. In the 14th century there were notable additions by Bishop Gower, a great builder, responsible also for the Palace. Later, fan vaulting in the Holy Trinity Chapel and a fine new oak nave ceiling. Subsequent neglect called forth a great last minute Victorian restoration by Sir Gilbert Scott, including a West Front by Scott based on de Leia's original, obliterating an 18th century restoration of John Nash.

There are interesting miserichords (see pic. p.30 of Sir Gawain being seasick), Saints' relics (David and Justinian possibly), and a good number of early Christian cross-incised stones at the back of the nave to be housed separately.

And don't forget the Bishop's Palace.

Whitesand to Caerfai

Distance and Time: 8½ m., 3¼ hrs.
Whitesand to Porthstinan: 2½ m., ¾ hr. walking.
St Justinian's (Porthstinan) to Porth Clais: 4 m.,
1¼ hrs.
Porth Clais to Caerfai: 2 m., ¾ hr.
The whole walk is divided into these three
sections purely for convenience. Each does, in
fact, make a good walk by itself.

Access and Condition of Path:

Car parking at Whitesand, Porthstinan, Porth
Clais and Caerfai. There is Fp. access at Porth-
sele, from Pencarnan; to the coast from Lower
Treginnis. For St Non's, the road (signposted in
St David's) goes past Warpool Court for ¼ mile
to the coast. Other Fp. as shown on the map.

Condition of the path is everywhere good;
sometimes extra care is needed.

Description:

The flat and windswept St David's peninsula
with its rocky outcrops, clustered farms and
sparse trees, has a curious fascination. It was the
end of the world for the medieval English and a
centre of Christianity before Canterbury.

The city of St David's is no more than a
village in size. It lies at the centre and roads
radiate to the coast.

Ramsey lies ¾ mile westwards across the
Sound. It is two miles long by a mile wide and
consists of 600 acres of rough, hilly but farmable

ldyn

ClegrFoia
Castell

Castell

Palace CATH.

St. Davids

Warpool
Court

r. Alun

St Nons
Chapel

Porth-
clais

St. Nons
Bay

Ca
fai
Ba

Trwyn-cynddeiriog

Carreg-
ran

land, now abandoned to the birds. Ask at Information Centres for
details of the few visits to be made. Trips round Ramsey daily in
summer from the lifeboat station. The seals and seabirds are
wonderful.

St Justinian, a Breton, built his cell on Ramsey about 500 A.D.
Legends abound: Justinian, having too many visitors, prayed that
the land bridge to the mainland would disappear. A giant axe then
chopped it to a series of rocks, called the Bitches, submerged at
high water and through which the tide runs with tremendous
force. Justinian had his head cut off and, decapitated, walked
across the Sound and laid his head on the spot now occupied by his
chapel at Porthstinan. The chapel post-dates him by about 1,000 years.

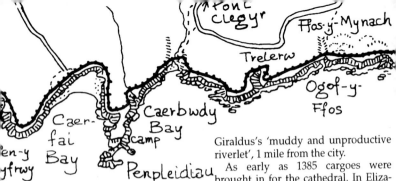

To the south-east of the chapel is the Saint's well. But unlike the well on Ramsey, there is no legend of healing attached to it.

A little to the south is Castell Heinif, an early Iron Age promontory fort with two banks: a 100-yard entrenchment cuts off a small promontory protected by steep cliffs.

Then a splendid walk, over two miles, round to Porthlysgi, on N.T. land. A Fp. joins from Treginnis. After Porth Maen Melyn, eastward to Porthlysgi. Lysgi was an early Irish raider. He landed, and killed Boia, a local Celtic chieftain who lived at Clegyr Boia, one mile inland. Small Iron Age hillfort on top. Neolithic house plan too; very rare.

Since Boia died about 520 A.D. he must have built on an earlier settlement. Boia's wife caused St. David much worry. Suspicious of the growing power of the monks, she told her maids (in the words of St. David's biographer) 'to go where the monks can see you and with bodies bare, play games and use lewd words'. But although the minds of the monks 'were enticed away to lust', St. David was unabashed and he fortified the resolution of his disciples.

Round the headland is Porth Clais, once the port for St David's, reached after 1¼ miles of rugged coast. It is at the mouth of the River Alun, Giraldus's 'muddy and unproductive riverlet', 1 mile from the city.

As early as 1385 cargoes were brought in for the cathedral. In Elizabethan times, timber came from Ireland and corn, malt and wool went to Bristol and Barnstaple.

The harbour wall has long been ruined and although coal was being brought here even after the war for the gasworks (now a car park), there wasn't much of a port after 1800. Small boats use the harbour now.

Twrch Trwyth, the fabulous boar with comb and scissors in his head, which King Arthur wanted, landed here from Ireland; you can find the full story in the Mabinogion.

All round is an abundance of wild flowers, especially in spring: thrift, squills, thyme, crowsfoot, campion.

St Non's Bay is next, after rounding Trwyncynddeiriog, so-called Mad Point from the prevailing gales. St Non was St David's mother; the medieval chapel in the field was dedicated to her. David was possibly born here about 462 A.D. in a great storm of thunder and lightning. At the Reformation, the chapel was converted into a cottage, the ground planted with leeks. An incised linear Latin ringcross, 7th century, is cut into a rough pillar-stone built into a wall of the chapel. The Holy Well close by, re-dedicated in 1951, was famed for curing rheumatism and eye ailments.

The large, conspicuous grey building was a Passionist monastery.

In ¾ mile you are at Caerfai Bay, past Pen y Cyfrwy (Saddle Head).

32

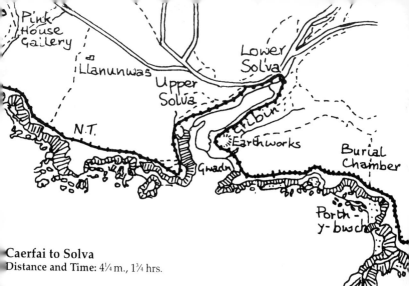

Caerfai to Solva
Distance and Time: 4¼ m., 1¾ hrs.

Access and Condition:
Car parking at Caerfai; on the road to Caerbwdy; and at Solva. There is a loop road from the main A427 at Pont Clegyr via Trelerw and rejoining further on. Roadside parking is difficult. Fp. at Caerbwdy, Trelerw, Llandruidion via Ffos y Mynach to the coast; from Nine Wells and Pink House to Porth y Rhaw; from Llanunwas to coast.

At the Solva end, you can walk either out on to the road and down the hill, or descend and walk along the foreshore to the car park via the harbour.

Description:
Caerfai is a fine sandy bathing beach with a good car park (and caravan site). Throughout the ages, the beautiful purple sandstone to build and repair the Cathedral has been quarried from Caerfai and Caerbwdy.

Between the two bays is a spectacular Iron Age fort, Penpleidiau, with four distinct banks cutting off the promontory.

Caerbwdy has sand only at low water. There are chocolate coloured rocks, an old mill site and lime kiln. On the western side of Caerbwdy, stone was quarried in 1972, but despite some local fears, no damage seems to have been done to the landscape.

There is a good wild stretch from Caerbwdy to Solva, mostly the rugged waste of Morfa Common, with inaccessible coves, rocky and stony, below. This area is now N.T.

At Ogof y Ffos begins the Ffos y Mynach, running north for three miles, ending in the north at Penbiri: possibly prehistoric or medieval: nobody knows.

East of Porth y Rhaw, a little cove, is a truly magnificent promontory fort, with dangerous looking cliffs to the east. At times one might scramble down but it is inadvisable.

The Council houses of upper Solva, typically on the skyline, tell you from afar where the village is.

33

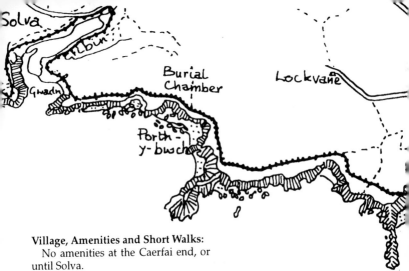

Village, Amenities and Short Walks:

No amenities at the Caerfai end, or until Solva.

Solva is the only village and an attractive one, too; formerly a fishing village and tiny port, now a tourist centre; lots of yachtsmen, and a rather English look in summer; popular for cottages and retirement. Shops, Post Office, good pubs and café; summer crowds; narrow street. Over the last generation, Solva has gone down hill a bit. Tourist influences are showing. Historically interesting as a port, with the best harbour in St Bride's Bay despite the dangerous entrance. There was an early trade with Wexford in cloth and timber; in the early 19th century there were 30 ships en route corn to Bristol, coal, culm and limestone brought in. But the last lime kiln, on the Gribin, was used in 1900.

Middle Mill, up the Solva valley is well worth a visit. It is one of the last three working mills in the county.

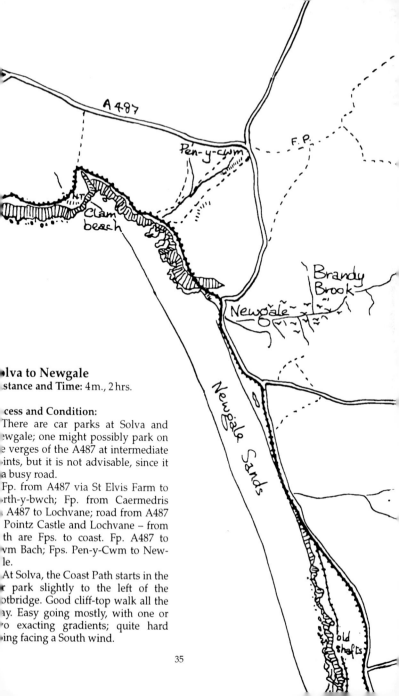

Solva to Newgale

Distance and Time: 4 m., 2 hrs.

Access and Condition:

There are car parks at Solva and Newgale; one might possibly park on the verges of the A487 at intermediate points, but it is not advisable, since it is a busy road.

Fp. from A487 via St Elvis Farm to Porth-y-bwch; Fp. from Caermedris on A487 to Lochvane; road from A487 to Pointz Castle and Lochvane – from both are Fps. to coast. Fp. A487 to Cwm Bach; Fps. Pen-y-cwm to Newgale.

At Solva, the Coast Path starts in the car park slightly to the left of the footbridge. Good cliff-top walk all the way. Easy going mostly, with one or two exacting gradients; quite hard going facing a South wind.

Description:

Up on the Gribin past the lime kilns; fine views and in season patches of pale blue squills, sea-pink, campions and violets. Ramsey far to the right, Skomer ahead, sewage works up the Cwm to the left, Gwadn beach below.

After an hour eastward along the path, the long headland of Dinas Fawr snakes out to sea. Coves and beaches below but inaccessible. Roch Castle far ahead, modern airfield building of Brawdy more prominent.

Not a specially good cliff for birds, an occasional kestrel apart. Gulls, jackdaws and occasional cormorants and fulmars; seals occasionally, too.

The long sandy expanse of Newgale lies ahead; backed by the thrown-up shingle bank. Rough cliff vegetation is colourful - gorse and heather, a carpet of squills; scabious and campion. The cliffs are craggy and jagged.

Worked flints from the Mesolithic to Bronze Age have been found in fields along this coast-line. Since it is in private land, exact locations have not been given here.

The only anti-climax is the exit at Newgale by little Bungalows.

Among the antiquities are the remains of two cromlechs south-west of St. Teilo's church, which itself is a pile of ruins in St. Elvis farmyard. Originally, Dinas Fawr and Dinas Fach were promontary forts. Pointz Castle, now a grassy hillock, was originally a mound castle of a Knight of Bishop de Leia(1176). Much of this land is now N.T. including St. Elvis.

Villages, Amenities and Short Walks:

No village at Newgale but shops, 'phone and pub at north end. Cafés and toilets at both ends of the beach. Short walks along the whole stretch of path using intermediate Fps. which are good.

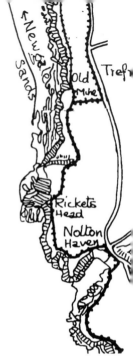

Newgale to Little Haven
Distance and Time:

Newgale (south) to Druidston: 3¾m., 1½h Druidston to Little Haven: 3m., 1¾hr

Access and Condition of Path:

Good car park at Newgale; and Nolton Haven, but not, please, on t beach. Limited parking on roadsi verges at Druidston; large car parks Broad Haven and Little Haven.

The path is good all the way but the are a couple of access places which a not quite so straightforward: fro Newgale you can either walk right alo the beach and make a very diffic scramble up the cliff (Trefrane Cliffs); better and safer, walk the narrow co road for 1¼ miles to the signpc Thence cliff-top to Nolton, 2 miles.

Across the Haven at Nolton on t road up by the Chapel, 1¼ miles Druidston, where you go left to t road from beach; ½ mile road, past Druidston Hotel, then back, by the signpost, across the field. Broad Haven after 2 miles, thence to Little Haven on the road, ¾ mile.

Description:

Pleasant, but not spectacular scenically. There are good short walks and plenty of parking. Unspectacular farmland away from the cliffs.

Scenically, there is a distinct softening of the landscape to the south, with the geological change from the older rocks of the St David's peninsula.

From Newgale to Druidston, rocks are the coal measures of Carboniferous times. Anthracite was mined here, but there is certainly no evidence except, south of Newgale, where the remains of a chimney and shafts of old Trefrane Colliery are still visible. Take care walking here.

Historically, a fascinating area; this is the beginning of Little England Beyond Wales; Brandy Brook at the north end of Newgale is the western end of the division between the Welshery in the North and the Englishry of the South of the county. The line ('Landsker', a Norse word) runs from Newgale via Roch, Camrose, Spittal, Llawhaden, Narberth down to Amroth on the Carmarthen border. Welsh to the north, English south.

Although there was an ethnic division in Norse times, the line was established by the Normans who invaded and held the south of the County. The line persisted in Elizabethan times (George Owen described it); and today, research done by Dr. Brian John has found astonishingly little change over a thousand years. Language, place-names, churches – all are different.

There are cliffs all the way, except for the cleft of Nolton Haven with its little beach and car park, hotel and a sprawling homely farm which seems to encompass the place. The 1¼m. from Druidston to Broad Haven are easy walking. The physical features have curiously splendid English names: Druidston and Haroldston Chins, Settling Nose. Druidston owes its name not to Druids but to a Norman knight, Drue, who invaded Ireland in the 12th century.

Villages, Amenities and Short Walks:

Nolton Haven has a pub, toilets and 'phone. Druidston has no amenities. Broad Haven is a large village, hotel, café, shops, garage, P.O., Countryside Unit, and YHA. Extensively developed. Little Haven has narrow hilly lanes, tiny roads, guest houses, P.O./Café, shops, craft shop and pottery, pubs. Road from Broad Haven to Little haven is narrow and dangerous.

Druidston Haven

Druidstone Chins

Haroldston Chins

Settling Nose

Harolds West

Harold Stone

Sleek Stone

car park

Broad Haven

Settland

Little Haven

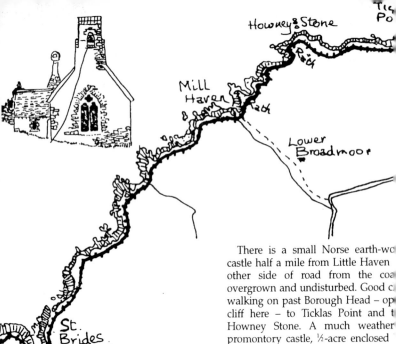

Little Haven to St Bride's
Distance and Time: 5¼m., 1¼hrs.

Access and Condition of Path:
Car parking at Little Haven and St Bride's; footpath access at Mill Haven, over halfway, via Lower Broadmoor Farm, but no vehicular access. A good path and quite easy walking all the way.

Description:
An attractive walk, especially the first half: relatively sheltered coast, low sheer cliffs by Little Haven, at times bracken and bramble clad, then by Goultrop Roads, you have the unusual experience of walking with a wood between you and the sea below: oak, ash, hazel, blackthorn, even pine: a pleasant change from open cliff-top, especially with the sound of the sea below.

There is a small Norse earth-wo castle half a mile from Little Haven other side of road from the coa overgrown and undisturbed. Good c walking on past Borough Head – op cliff here – to Ticklas Point and t Howney Stone. A much weather promontory castle, ½-acre enclosed two lines of banks. A ¼m. south-w of this is another cliff fort – Broadmc or Mill Haven camp, where 1½ ac are enclosed by a convex rampart a ditch. ('Rath' on O.S. map.)

Just here the rocks change dramat ally: from Pre-Cambrian to Old R Sandstone – the cliffs and path and ploughed fields all become rich a red instead of weathered grey.

Birds to watch out for all along path are the Gulls – Herring, Blac backed; Fulmars; Ravens, Cormoran Shags, Oyster-catchers.

Being on the coast, you fortunate miss the nasty dereliction of Talben airfield, still an inheritance of Wo War Two.

Villages and Amenities:
Toilets at St. Brides and a phone ju up the road at the junction. Restor medieval (12 or 13 C.) church and fi lime kiln.

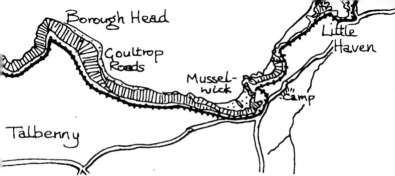

t Bride's to Marloes Sands South)

Distance and Time: 7 m., 3 hrs.
t Bride's to Musselwick Sands: 2 m.,
hr.
Musselwick Sands to Martin's Haven:
¼ m., ½-hour.
Martin's Haven round Deer Park:
½ m., ½-hour
Martin's Haven to Marloes Sands (Fp.
) car park): 1¼ m., ¾-hour; then ½ m.,
nore to Three Chimneys (end of map).

Access and Condition:
Car parking at St Bride's, and at
Martin's Haven and Marloes car parks.
e considerate, don't park on the slip-
vay at Martin's Haven, even though
kindivers do. Footpath access at
Musselwick Sands; road-side parking
nd path across farmer's fields; on
earing beach take left hand path for
'oast Path. The path is good all the
vay; this section is fine walking. but
parking is difficult.

Description:
Flat, exposed walk past St Bride's.
'hen to Nab Head, where there was a
Neolithic Flint factory (flints now in
enby Museum). A hundred yards
urther on is Tower Point, a big
promontory fort. Two sides are
reciptous cliffs, the neck is defended
y a rampart; a bank and a ditch, one
roded, the other silted up.
Martin's Haven is embarkation
point for Skomer, 10.00am, 11.00am
and 12 noon daily in summer, a pebbly
little cove sheltered from the S.W. and a
couple of miles west of Marloes. The
promontory beyond the crumbling
high stone wall is the Deer Park.
Incised ring-cross in the wall near the
cottage. Iron Age promontory camp on
the hill. Renny Slip, on the south side
of Martin's Haven, is a good little
sandy beach. National Trust Car Park.
The sea round Skomer has been made
into a marine Nature Reserve.

The wildness and exposed nature of
the coast is somewhat softened by the
presence of the islands. Both Skomer,
directly west and Skokholm, to the
south, were farmed, but are now en-
tirely devoted to bird-watching. Both
are National Nature Reserves,
administered by the West Wales Wildlife Trust and are internationally
celebrated for their sea-bird colonies:
Gulls, Petrels, Shearwaters, Puffins,
Razorbills, Guillemots. Access
restricted at Skokholm. Most of the
mainland of the peninsula here is
owned by the National Trust, and the
West Wales Wildlife Trust has
prepared a Nature Trail leaflet (ask at
Information Centres). Fp. starts at the
Marloes car park (1 mile beyond
village).

Fine Iron Age promontory fort at
Gateholm where three banks and
ditches defend the accessible side.
Gateholm has numerous hut circles

and enclosures; flints and pottery have been found. It is not really an island since it is accessible at low water.

Marloes Sands, one of the finest expanses anywhere; Old Red Sandstone deposited on Silurian rocks, some 400 million years ago, upended the later faulted and contorted sea stacks. The flat-topped interior here was also produced by sea erosion; the 'wave-cut' platform was produced when the sea-level was 200ft. higher. Marloes Beacon, volcanic rock, was then a small island stack in the sea.

Grey seals can often be seen round Martin's Haven and the Deer Park: pups too, especially in October in the small bays.

Don't confuse National Trust and National Park. The National Trust is private organisation owning land an houses to preserve them. The Nationa Park is a name only for a beautifu area which it is hoped, somehow, wi be preserved.

Village amenities and Short Walks:

Marloes is the only village; pub P.O. and shop, refreshments, accom modation and meals. Double bellcote Celtic type church, restored.

Car park and toilets at Martin' Haven.

Youth Hostel down near Nationa Trust car park for Marloes Sands.

The N.T. car park is a good centra point for short walks: St Bride's t Musselwick Sands; Musselwick Sand to Martin's Haven round the Dee Park; Marloes National Trust car par to Martin's Haven.

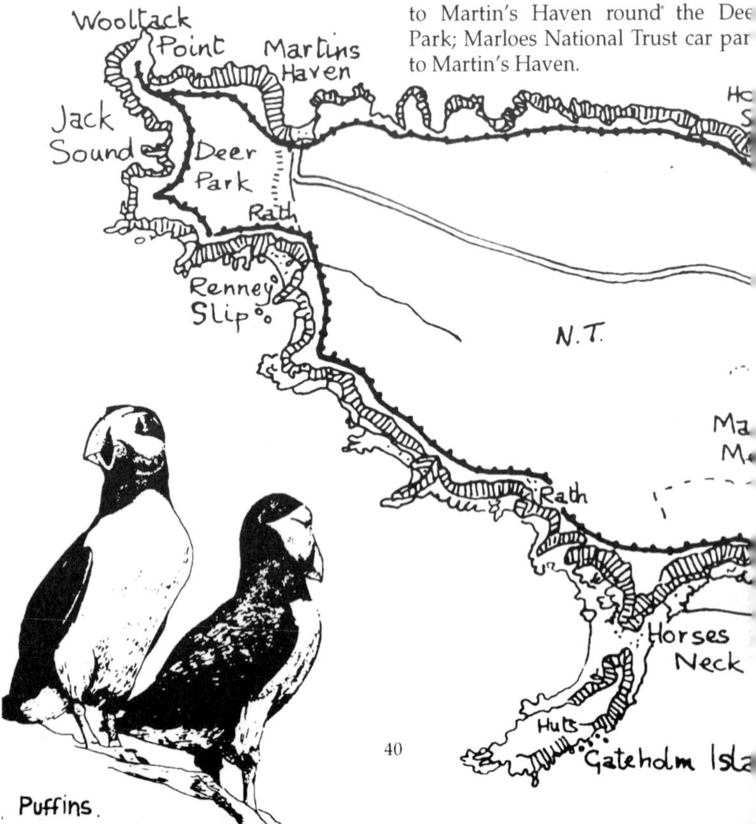

Puffins.

40

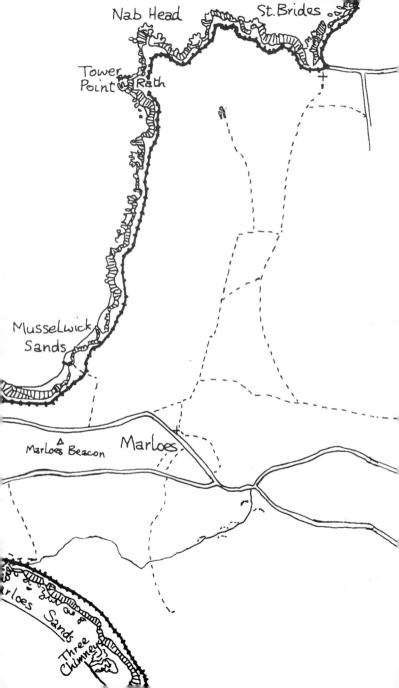

Marloes Sands to St Ann's Head

Distance and Time: 3½m., 1¼hrs.
Marloes Sands to Westdale Bay (Fp.) 1½m., ½hr.
Westdale Bay to St Ann's Head 2¼m., 1hr.

Access and Condition of Path:
Car Parking in National Trust Car Park at Marloes and at Kete. Fp. from Dale to Westdale Bay (opposite church, up lane). Access to beach. Path good most of the way.

Description:
The 200ft. 'wave-cut platform' makes a fine walk, sheer cliffs of Old Red Sandstone, small bays; scarred by the remains at Kete of Royal Naval Air Station. In 1967 the National Trust bought the land from roughly West-dale Bay to St Ann's Head with funds from Enterprise Neptune.

Immediately south of Westdale Bay at Great Castle Head is a fine promontory fort, Iron Age, with two ramparts and banks, enclosing the headland. But you must be careful along this grassy windswept path: the Old Red Sandstone cliffs are sheer at times and the path may be crumbling.

At St. Ann's Head detour to Cobbler Hole view point for beautiful foldin of the rocks.

Short Walks:
Marloes Sands and Kete are goc points for starting from. Several sho walks possible from Kete. Also roun the whole peninsula.

St Ann's Head to Sandy Haven

Distance and Time: 9 or 11¼m roughly: 4¼ or 5¼hrs.
St Ann's head to Watwick Bay: (Fp 1¾m., ¾hr.
Watwick to Dale village: 1 3/4 m., ¾hr.
Dale (Griffin Inn) to Monk Haven:
    at low water 2¼m., 1 hr.
    at high water 2¼ miles more.
Monk Haven to Great Castle Head 1¾m., 1hr. Great Castle Head to Sand Haven: 1¼m., ¾hr.

Access and Condition of Path:
There is car parking in Dale villag at Pickleridge, in St Ishmael's, at Mon Haven, down a lovely wooded roa and Sandy Haven, though the latter pretty restricted. At the other acces

42

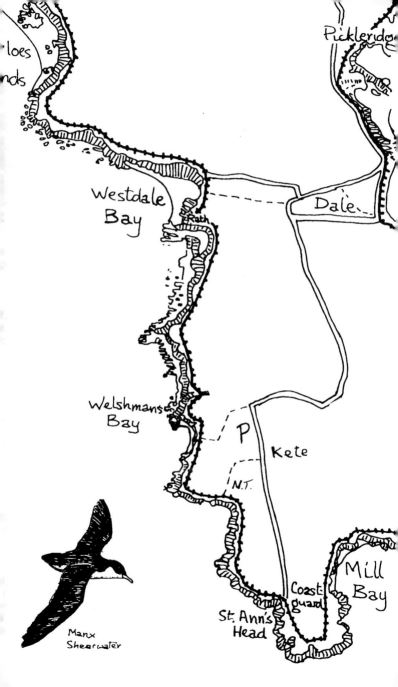

Pickleridge

loes
nds

Westdale
Bay

Rath

Dale

Welshmans
Bay

P

Kete

N.T.

Mill
Bay

Coast
guard

St. Ann's
Head

Manx
Shearwater

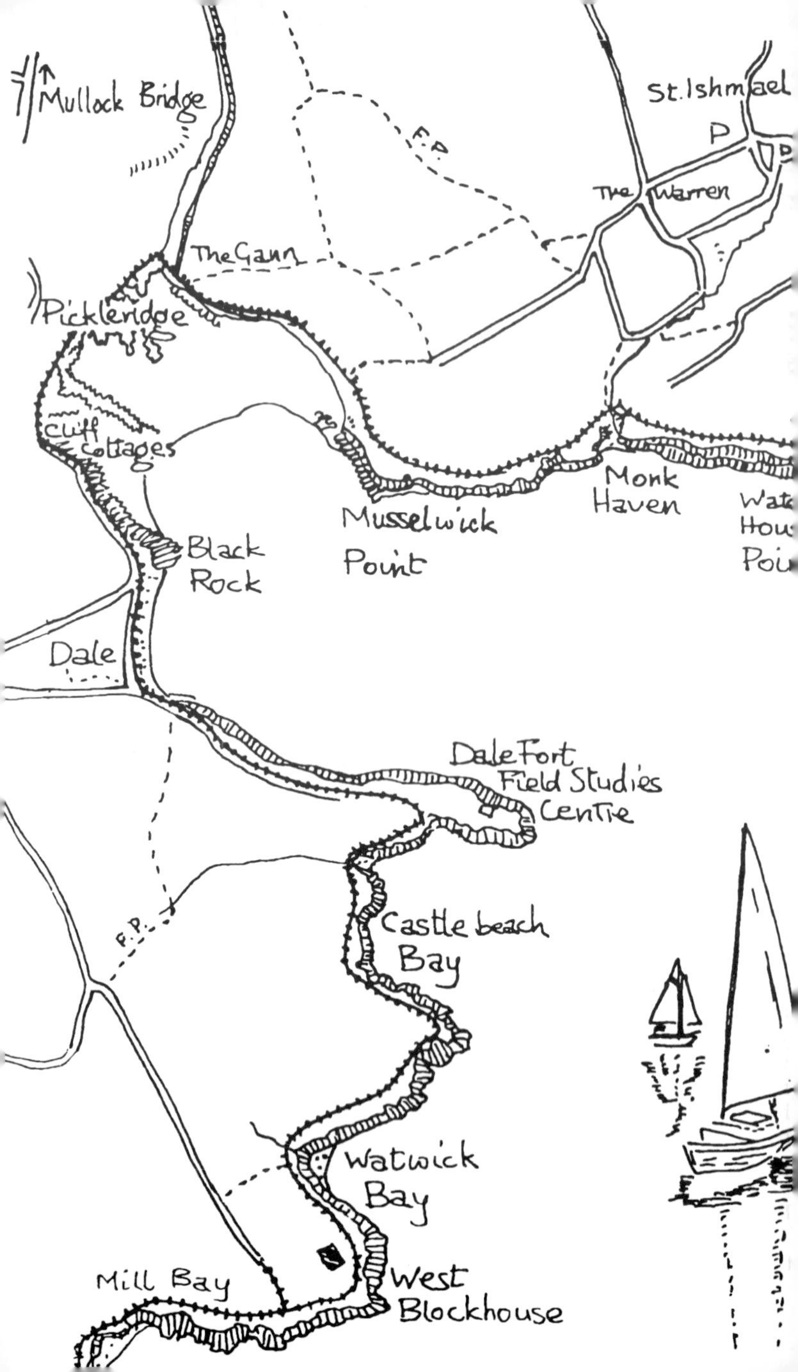

Mullock Bridge

St. Ishmael
P
D
The Warren

The Gann

Pickleridge

Cliff Cottages

Musselwick Point

Monk Haven

Water House Point

Black Rock

Dale

F.P.

Dale Fort Field Studies Centre

Castle beach Bay

F.P.

Watwick Bay

Mill Bay

West Blockhouse

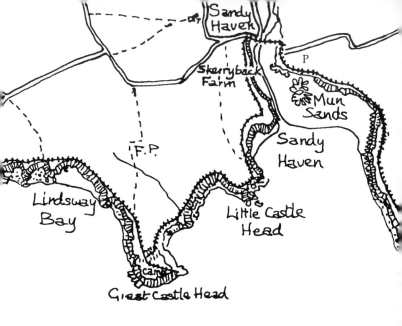

points, it is roadside verge parking which in summer is very limited.

From St Ann's Head to Dale, path good. The path at Dale can be tricky. At low water simply go from Cliff Cottages across the Saltings at Pickleridge to The Gann (stepping stones across river); then keep on the beach to Musselwick. At high water you have to make a long detour; walk up the road to Mullock Bridge, continue over and come down the Fp. at Mullock to Musselwick. You can go right round by road to Trewarren at St Ishmael's and then to Monk Haven. Actually, you can cross two hours before low water at The Gann and at Sandy Haven (see next page) a couple of hours after, so allowing up to two hours walking, you can manage without going round by road.

Description:

St. Ann's Head to Dale, completes the Dale peninsula, a good walk; Dale to Musselwick, by contrast, is across mud flats; then a cliff walk to Monk Haven, then a fine rocky coast, past Great Castle Head to Sandy Haven.

At Mill Bay, Henry Tudor, Duke of Richmond, landed in 1485, went on to collect an army and won the Crown of England at Bosworth, a fortnight later, becoming Henry VII, the first Welsh King of England.

West Blockhouse was an early Tudor fort; Dale Fort was a Victorian fort, a belated defence of Milford Haven, outlined in more detail later. Dale Fort is now a Field Centre. On Dale Point is an Iron Age promontory fort. The peninsula is a fine farming area with a great reputation for early crops.

Villages, Amenities and Short Walks:

Dale, like Marloes cannot be called an architecturally distinguished village, the local homes are mostly Admiralty and Local Authority type. Animated in summer by a swollen

population for sailing. Pub, shop, P.O., sailing club and chandler. Dale Castle, rebuilt on an ancient site, is not open to the public.

St. Ishmael's is a spread-out and rambling village.

The church down at Monk Haven, as its name implies, was used in the times of the early Christian travellers; a Celtic type, bell-coted with no tower, dark and pleasant in a most attractive setting. Shop, P.O., pub in St. Ishmael's, not Monk Haven, the latter has nothing.

Sandy Haven to Milford
Distance and Time:
Sandy Haven to South Hook Point: 1¾m., 1hr.
South Hook Point to Gelliswick: 1m., ½hr.
Gelliswick to Milford (road): 1¾m., ½hr.

Access and Condition of Path:
Car Park in private field east side of Sandy Haven (small charge); otherwise turning bay only. Parking at Gelliswick, Milford and Mun Sands (Sandy Haven beach), signposted from Herbrandston. The path is adequate everywhere, much is on road anyway.

One can cross at Sandy Haven at low water, (see previous page). Otherwise by a long road detour.

Description.
This is not the wild coast of the north of Dale; but one of the attractions of Pembrokeshire scenery is its variety and the change from the quiet solitude of Monk Haven to the modern technology of the oil refineries is striking, though, since the disappearance of Esso, the scene is desolation rather than industry.

The Haven itself is splendid, but for those who walk to enjoy the countryside, from here on it's rather a duty, and a speculation on what might have been. But the historical interest abides.

Mun's Mouth was, according to Fenton, where the Flemings first landed, some 800 years ago, "in a small creek at the bottom of the little dingle."

The Haven was claimed by Nelson as the finest natural harbour in Europe. A drowned river valley, geologically called a 'Ria', it has an

46

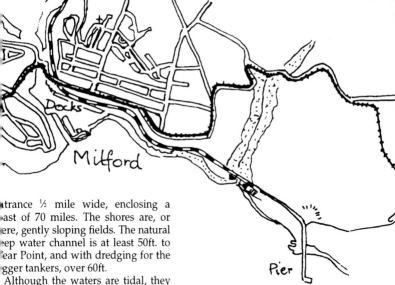

entrance ½ mile wide, enclosing a coast of 70 miles. The shores are, or were, gently sloping fields. The natural deep water channel is at least 50ft. to Wear Point, and with dredging for the bigger tankers, over 60ft.

Although the waters are tidal, they are calm and slow – 2 knots below Wear Point – but with a consequent silting in the Pembroke, Carew, Cresswell and Sandy Haven estuaries.

Despite the Norse, Hubba with his 3 ships, and the late Norman invasions of both here and Ireland via the Haven, there is surprisingly little history of activity on the northern side; indeed, there was no port until 1800, when Milford was built.

Sir William Hamilton inherited the Manors of Hubberston and Pill from his first wife, a Barlow of Slebech. His nephew the Hon. Charles Greville acting as his agent, literally built the new port. Quaker whalers from Nantucket in New England, who were refugees from the American Revolution, were encouraged to establish whaling and shipbuilding. Jean Louis Baraillier, a dockyard constructor from Toulon, supervised.

The town was laid out in blocks, the main streets running parallel and intersected. Greville put everything he had into the development, even transferring Emma, his 'fair tea-maker' to his uncle for money to continue. On a memorable occasion in 1802, Lord Nelson himself came with Emma and Sir Williams Hamilton and Greville and celebrated.

The Admiralty took a hand with shipbuilding and later they wanted to buy, but they wouldn't be held to ransom and in 1814 when Greville's heir wanted too much, they took their business across the Haven and built their own dockyard at Pembroke Dock. The advent of gas adversely affected the whaling – the oil was used for street lighting – and the decline of Milford increased when the hoped-for transatlantic liner traffic never came. Milford was a leading deep-sea fishing port, though that too had waned after the Second W. W., until fortunes were restored by oil ten years ago.

Esso in 1960, then BP in 1962, Texaco 1966, Gulf in 1968, and finally Amoco in 1971 have all set up terminals and in most cases refineries too.

But the Oil Companies have fallen on hard times. Esso has been dismantled; BP has closed. Sic transit …!

47

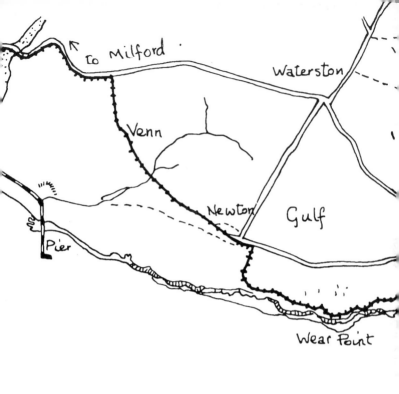

Before North Sea Oil, everything was planned on the basis of bringing very large quantities of crude oil from the Middle East and the Gulf. Milford Haven was chosen, as a natural deep water harbour, for the enormous VLCC (Very Large Crude Carriers), up to 250,000 tons. These are now like dinosaurs and industry is reverting to small tankers going to small ports with their own refining capacity near their markets.

The forts along the haven have historical interest. East Blockhouse at Angle and West Blockhouse remain as ruins from Tudor times. Despite subsequent surveys, it needed the advent of steam shipping and the Naval Dockyard in the 19th century to give the impetus to defence. General Gordon, when an Engineer Lieutenant, had prepared plans. Some dozen forts were built between 1850 and 1870. Never used, they became rapidly out-of-date. Most are now derelict, though Dale is a Field Study Centre and Thorn Island an hotel. They were conceived as a group and while each was self-supporting with its own garrison, they covered each other.

Neyland

Hazelbeach Llanstadwell

coast path undefined until south of Haven

Toll
Bridge

To Pembroke Dock

Milford to Pembroke Dock

Distance and Time:
From Milford 1½m., ½hr. on the Neyland Road, lane entrance of Venn Farm, Fp (C.P. sign, right). Fp, Road via Hazelbeach.

Access and Condition of Path:
Car Parking at Milford and Neyland and in between at Hazel-beach and Llanstadwell. Easy walking.

Description:
It is all relative; this is pleasant enough walking, even picturesque in parts, but the siting of Gulf at Waterston seems designed to give everyone the maximum impact of life at an oil refinery. It is the epitome of bad planning.

Flat and rural countryside, semi-industrialised with the beginning of rural sprawl, more to come probably. So you're in for a long haul by road in uninteresting landscape.

Villages and Amenities:
Neyland: like Milford is a recent growth. It was chosen by the great engineer, Isambard Brunel, as a terminus for the South Wales-Manchester railway. It then became a terminal for the Irish Packet Service to Waterford, but in 1906, Fishguard took over, and the fishing fleet went to Milford.

You can walk either up through the town or, unofficially, along past the Marina, scramble up the bank on to the road and walk over the Bridge.

After a long spell in the doldrums, Neyland is looking up. A new Marina has brought activity and the houses have been brightened up. But, the Coast Path has lengthened. Instead of taking the ferry from Neyland, you now have to walk past the Marina, scramble up the bank on to the road, walk over the bridge, and on to the main Cleddau Bridge. There's parking space on both the Neyland and Burton sides of the Pill. Unless you are a real glutton for punishment, skip walking between Neyland and Pembroke.

Pembroke to Bentlass

Distance and Time: Bridge to Pembroke Castle: 2 m., ¾ hr.
Pembroke Castle to Bentlass: 1½ m., ½ hr.

Access and Condition of Path:

Car Parking is good and plentiful in Pembroke Dock, and in Pembroke itself. Room for roadside parking at Monkton, Hundleton or Bentlass (limited). You can cut out Pembroke Dock or take time out to visit – it is a very pleasant town. By road through Pembroke and Monkton to unclassified road where Fp. branches off. Stone stile, quite hard to find, and boggy patch leads to Fp. The walking is easy though.

Pembroke Dock is an example of early 19th century town planning, though this is not apparent unless you take time off to wander round it. In 1814 it became a Royal Dockyard town, like Portsmouth and Chatham, until the docks closed in 1926.

All the Royal yachts and many fine armoured cruisers were built here. The town suffered in the Care and Maintenance days after 1926. But in World War Two, it became the world's largest flying boat base, though now, alas, even the last Sunderland is gone.

The town was planned on a grid system with wide streets and much working-class Georgian and Regency architecture is still intact, and it looks better than its modern counterpart.

Monkton is really a suburb of Pembroke. The parish church was the Priory church founded, with Castle, by the Norman Arnulf de Montgomery. It has been well and extensively restored, but its spaciousness reflects its medieval past. Close by is Monkton Old Hall, a private well-restored 15th century house, originally the Prior's home. Animal and human remains, as well as Bronze Age implements – a saw and chisel – were found in a cave near Monkton Bridge; now in the National Museum of Wales.

Milford, Neyland and Pembroke Dock are all-of-a-piece Victorian, or a

50

least 19th century. Pembroke itself is very different. It is of all ages. The town grew up in the 13th century, after the rebuilding by the powerful Marcher Earls of the formidable castle, which was the fact and symbol of their strength and presence. It was the one impregnable one too, for it was never taken by the Welsh, though they almost starved the garrison out in

has an Inner and Outer Ward and a splendid Norman Keep, rare in Britain being circular and 100 feet high, four stories and a basement. Below is the huge Wogan cavern, a natural cavern 70 by 50 feet reached by steps from the Keep or by boat from the Pembroke river.

In the second Civil War, Cromwell himself besieged and afterwards

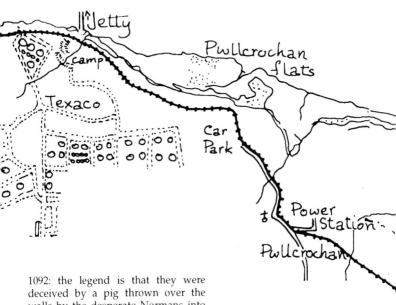

1092: the legend is that they were deceived by a pig thrown over the walls by the desperate Normans into thinking supplies were plentiful. It sounds a bit unlikely, but they may have been more gullible in those days. The first Tudor king, Henry VII, was born there. The Earls of Pembroke do not live there now, the castle is in the competent hands of a Trust (small admission charge).

The strategic position of the castle is very sound; water on three sides, and the castle fills its limestone promontory. It was built about 1100; it

destroyed the gateway and most of the Outer Ward, leaving a shell. Then followed two hundred years of neglect before the work of restoration.

Make a detour up the Main Street the architectural variety is pleasing and the contrast between the Castle at one end and the Methodist Chapel at almost the other is striking. One of the churches, St Mary's, is 13th century and the other, St Michael's, is 19th.

Bentlass to Texaco Car Park
Distance and Time: 3¾ m., 1¼ hrs.

Access and Condition of Path:

Roadside parking with very great difficulty at the beginning; Texaco car park in field at the commencement of the Coast Path. No access by the Jetty. There is a stretch on the road near the beginning and from the Power Station to Pwllcrochan.

Straightforward easy Fp. walking to the jetty: after that, the uncared for path is very hard going.

Description:

This seems a most unpromising stretch to look at since much of it is round the Power Station and the last mile or more is within Texaco's land, concrete posts and wire fence.

But in fact it is quite enjoyable, especially as far as Lambeeth. The unclassified roads from Monkton to Hundleton and then on to Pwllcrochan past Goldborough and Lambeeth farms are delightful, rural and unspoilt, back fifty years from Power and Oil.

You will see the first Coast Path sign in the cwm past Whym Cottage, and it leads to Lambeeth, where you go through the farmyard past the 18th century farmhouse and on through the Power Station, by the tip and out on the road.

From Lambeeth on, there is not much enjoyment, it is true, but the Power Station is at least imposing and until you get to Texaco there should be no smell of oil.

From the Car Park to the Jetty – and further – it is typical Haven scenery – sloping banks, bracken, blackthorn, down to the water's edge with fields to the slope. The soil, as one can see from its colour, is of the Old Red Sandstone. Lots of sheep, so keep dogs on a lead.

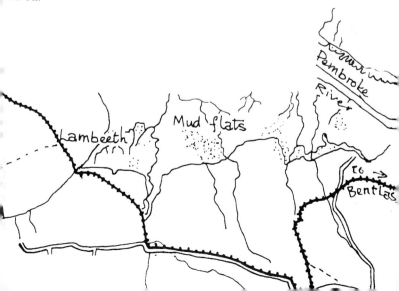

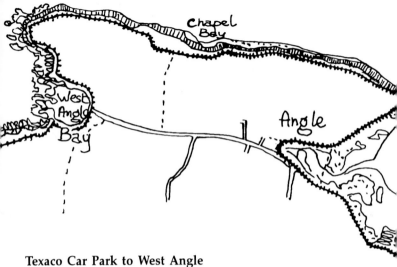

Texaco Car Park to West Angle Bay

Distance and Time:

Texaco Car Park to Angle Point: 5½m., 2¼hrs.

Angle Point to West Angle Bay: 2m., ¾hr.

Access and Condition of Path:

This walk divides into two sections; the starting point, at Texaco, is on the previous map. Parking for a few cars at Texaco Berth No. 6 at Angle Bay.

Car Parking in Angle village, you can drive out to near the Point, where the pub is; good Car Park at West Angle Bay.

Few Fps., there is one to just west of Chapel Bay, a lane, but not signposted either end. One Fp. south of West Angle Bay to the East Blockhouse Road.

The path is good except for round Bullwell Bay. A couple of hundred yards east of the Popton Fort, the roadway ends, and the path is hard to see through undergrowth in the wood and long grass in the fields. If it were walked more often, it would be better, but walkers can be excused for not making this their favourite stretch. Ocean terminal BP has now closed down and the jetty once used to import the crude oil is now redundant.

Fort Popton was left empty by BP but it now contains a Field Studies Council Research Centre. This is hardly a sympathetic place for walking but the asphalt surface on the BP road is something to be thankful for – and pleasanter than the subsequent foreshore.

Industry doesn't seem to last. As oil installations become out-dated, so the companies pull in their horns and retire to England, let's hope they take their pollution with them.

Description

The beginning, to Sawdern Point, is of the same quality as the last stretch,

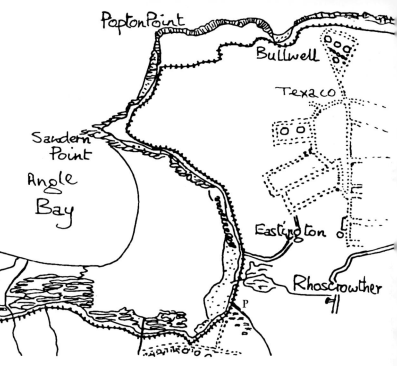

then, in the little Angle peninsula, one feels somehow more isolated. The soil is still the same deep red sandstone, but one is even more struck by the windswept aspect, and the clumps are whale-backed by the gales.

The bay is a vast mud and sand flatness and Angle straggles in an idiosyncratic way. An attractive church (red roof apart), a miniature fishermen's chapel, remains of a 14th century tower; 15th century dovecote.

The two forts – Popton, which one walks around, and Thorn Island, are mid-Victorian.

Before Angle, you may notice Eastington, a corruption of Jestynton (a Normanising of Iestyn), a 14th century square peel-tower type manor house now in with the farm.

This is an area of great estates and, formerly, great families: Meyricks of Bush, Owens of Orielton, Lorts and later Campbells of Stackpole. Now it's the oil companies, the National Trust, the Ministry of Defence, sharing the land with the private Angle estate. But Stackpole Court has been demolished, the Army has Castlemartin, and Orielton is split up. Orielton House is now a Field Centre specialising in Marine Biology and keeping a sharp research eye on oil pollution.

Villages, Amenities and Short Walks:
Angle has accommodation, hotel, shops, pubs Manor Hall. Very much the grouped village of England rather than the dispersed Welsh hamlet. Café, toilets and 'phone at West Angle Bay. Short walk from Angle to West Angle Bay and back along the road, or halfway to Chapel Bay then to the road.

West Angle Bay to Freshwater West

Distance and Time: 4½m., 2½hrs.

Access and Condition of Path:

This was the last stretch of the Coast Path to be made up. There was no existing right of way and the land-owner and farmers did not want to grant one. Finally, after an enquiry, the Government designated a path.

Car parking is good at each end, but there are no intermediate access paths and no signposts anywhere, or stiles. Not for young children, dogs or the elderly, and no bare legs and sandals.

There are a couple of fields at the start then the open cliff all the way.

Description:

This is scenically as exciting as, and possibly more satisfying than, the Red Sandstone cliffs of the Dale peninsula, coming as it does after the soft land-scapes of the Haven.

Open cliff by the R.A.F. installation and down to East Blockhouse, the Tudor remains of an early defence fort. Rat Island has a fine colony of formidable Greater Black Backed Gulls, and Choughs, which are not so often seen as on the northern coasts.

Although George Owen in 1603 ascribed the Blockhouse to Henry VIII, Fenton thought the Romans had possibly started something there.

Superb cliff scenery, craggy and contorted red rocks. Sad reminders of the War at intervals: derelict look-out huts, rusty stanchions, concrete, rusty iron, but it is not the blight on the landscape modern bungalows would have been.

Half a mile or so further, there is a fine promontory fort on the mainland by Sheep Island. This is Skomer Neck Camp at Castles Bay. A bank and ditch cut off half an acre and a natural gully cuts off the rest of the promon-tory, a couple of acres.

There was a tower there in Eliza-bethan times, traditionally a place of refuge for Norman raiders, but more likely Norse according to Fenton.

A steep scramble down to the stony beach can be found at Whitedole Bay.

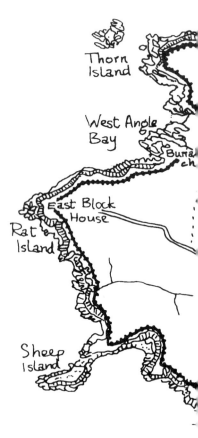

Fenced to the edge, gorse to seaward a bit further and one or two boggy patches, but nothing to worry about, though from West Pickard Bay the mat of low gorse and bramble intertwined is formidable. From a distance it looks simply brackeny, but it isn't.

Another promontory fort between West and East Pickard Bay; banks to the north and east, cliffs to the west, entrance to the south-east.

Inland from here was the war-time Angle Airfield, and the B4320 runs half a mile inland.

What makes this possibly a better walk in winter than summer is that you may easily see a field of lapwings or curlews, and the sea-birds are even more numerous.

End up on the sand at Freshwater West, one of the two finest stretches of sand in the County (Marloes is the other). A large part of the dunes here are N.T. There is a fine large boulder of rough Conglomerate, Nature's own concrete, which you will have to walk past to get to the road. This is not a beach for bathing.

Villages, Amenities and Short Walks:

No villages. Cafe, toilets and telephone at West Angle Bay. Few short walks owing to absence of Fps. From West Angle Bay to East Block-house (½hr.) and back is good.

Freshwater West to Stack Rocks
Distance and Time: 5½m., 1½hrs.

Access and Condition of Path:

All on the road. As far as Castle-martin much of it is the Military range boundary and from Castlemartin on, it is within the Range. At Ermigate Lane, the road from Warren to the coast, you turn to Flimston, or what is left of it, ending at Stack Rocks.

Car parks at each end of this stretch and at the beginning of Ermigate Lane. Roadside parking elsewhere.

Description

This road walk is the official 'Coast Path'. There is no indication that one will ever be able to walk freely round the coast, well-known as being one of the finest limestone cliffs in Britain, below a flat-topped platform of a land-scape. Good walk even on the road.

Seaweed (purple laver) drying hut at the end of Freshwater West. Made of driftwood roofed by reed (originally Marram Grass) and ridged with turf. Restored by the National Park Authority. Owned by the N.T.

The Green Bridge of Wales, a natural wave-cut arch is just to the west of the Car Park at Stack Rocks.

It is not just a whim on the part of the military that closes off the coast to the west: said to be dangerous with unexploded missiles. But to the east the path is open when there is no

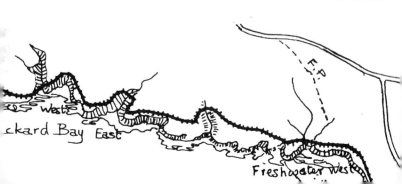

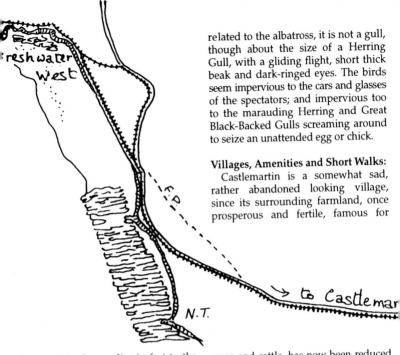

Freshwater West

F.P.

→ to Castlemar

N.T.

related to the albatross, it is not a gull, though about the size of a Herring Gull, with a gliding flight, short thick beak and dark-ringed eyes. The birds seem impervious to the cars and glasses of the spectators; and impervious too to the marauding Herring and Great Black-Backed Gulls screaming around to seize an unattended egg or chick.

Villages, Amenities and Short Walks:

Castlemartin is a somewhat sad, rather abandoned looking village, since its surrounding farmland, once prosperous and fertile, famous for

firing – this also applies in fact to the road down to Stack Rocks. As well as a road notice, warnings are given in the local press.

The celebrated Stack Rocks, Flimston Stacks or Elegug Stacks, are two huge pillars of detached limestone, a stone's throw from the cliff edge. Elegug is the Welsh for Guillemot and it is the name used in South Pembrokeshire too. Here are the finest seabird colonies to be seen from the path anywhere, especially in the first half of the year. The top and broad ledges below are packed with Guillemots. Razor-bills lower in the crevices and under overhands. Guillemots have more pointed beaks and are a deep chocolate brown to the Razor-bills' black.

There are little Kittiwake Gulls on extraordinarily sheer rock. Fulmar Petrels nest here on the cliffs too –

corn and cattle, has now been reduced to desert, with sheep from the Preselies wandering among fenceless fields. The village has an unusual and rare 18th century round, stone cattle pound. An attempt to remove the pound in the interests of greater road speed was happily thwarted.

The church, ½ mile north of the village, is 13th century with the usual battlemented tower; in the churchyard are the ruins of 'The Old Vicarage', including a 12th century arcade.

This is a very different area from a generation ago.

It's now a favourite cliff climbing locale. There's a National Park leaflet saying where and when you can and can't climb the cliffs. Unless you're an expert, don't.

And now the Army too has produced a leaflet, justifying their turning the peninsula into a waste land.

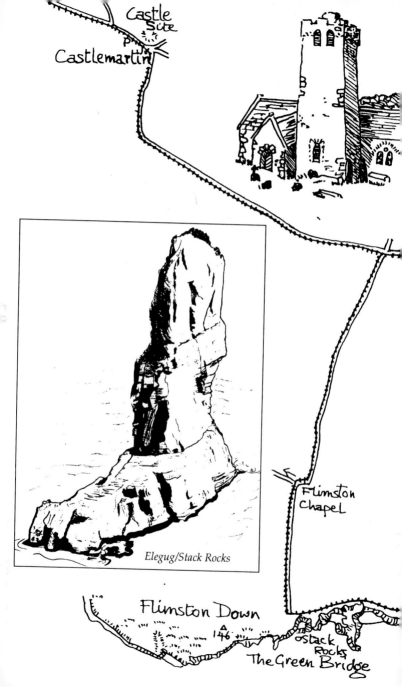

Castle Site

Castlemartin

Flimston Chapel

Flimston Down

△ 146

Stack Rocks

The Green Bridge

Elegug/Stack Rocks

Stack Rocks to Broad Haven

Distance and Time: 4m., 2hrs., 2m. extra via Bosherston and road to Trefalen.

Access and Condition of Path:

Car Parking at each end, Stack Rocks and Broad Haven (small charge), above St Govan's Chapel, and roadside parking, if available, in Bosherston village, which is often crowded in summer. No intermediate access; mostly Ministry of Defence land.

Until recently, one had to walk from St Govan's Chapel by road round to Boshertson and thence by road via Trefalen to Broad Haven, an annoying gap in the path between St Govan's Chapel and Broad Haven direct; even more annoying for those at Broad Haven who wanted to walk to St Govan's. Then the Army voluntarily released the path through, and up to St Govan's Head. There are the usual safeguards – they reserve the right to close it, but in practice, you will usually find it open.

The condition of the path is good everywhere.

Description:

If one is denied the walk west from Stack Rocks, then we can be appreciative of this one: a fine stretch on flat open cliff above splendid sheer Carboniferous Limestone cliffs.

The level cliff-top is wave action, and so are the many caves, blowholes, isolated stacks, arches and inlets. Birds apart from those mentioned at Stack Rocks, are Ravens, Shags, Martins, Jackdaws in number, Oystercatchers and Choughs. The wild flowers are beautiful, particularly the blue squills and the sea lavender.

Immediately east of Stack Rocks is Flimston Castle, a peninsula, caves below and an Iron Age promontory fort with stony banks enclosing the 150 feet deep Cauldron. Traces of a track down the cliff to a natural harbour. The twenty five foot rise and fall of the tides and tremendous currents

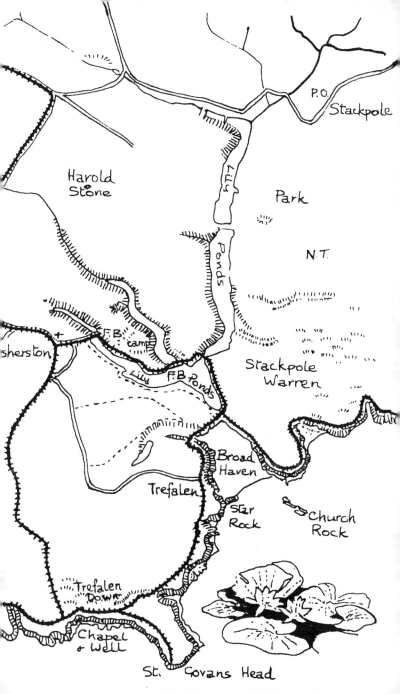

P.O.
Stackpole

Harold
Stone

Park

N.T.

Lily

Ponds

Stackpole
Warren

sherston

+

F.B.
camp

Lily

F.B. Ponds

Broad
Haven

Trefalen

Star
Rock

Church
Rock

Trefalen
Down

Chapel
& Well

St. Govans Head

under the cliffs must have presented problems to prehistoric sailors.

Half a mile further is Crocksydam Camp, another fort, defended on three sides by cliffs, and on the landward by a rampart and ditch. The Castle on Buckspool Down, 1 mile further, is yet another promontory fort; a rampart and ditch across the neck of land, and steep cliffs either side. At Newton Down, 1 mile more, is Bosherston Mere, a huge cleft; here is the Huntsman's Leap. Not, perhaps, too difficult, but the sea is there 130ft. below. The legendary huntsman after jumping it, went back unwisely and never rode again, dying of nightmares into the bargain.

The highlight of the walk is probably St Govan's Chapel, a small, rough, single-chamber, stone cell dating from the 13th century. It is down 52 rough stone steps. It is dark and damp, an empty bell-cote, a stone altar at the east end, a single slit above. There is a well below the chapel, protected by a stone hood. It was famous for healing, though it is dry

now. Nobody knows who St Gov was: the Arthurian Gawaine of t Round Table; Goven, wife of a Cel King; Gobham, Irish contemporary St David. As far as Malkin, in the 18 century was concerned, there was question, it was Sir Gawaine with Gawaine's Head beyond. Just east St Govan's Head is New Quay, an o harbour. The Army forbids us to down though.

Bosherston Lily Ponds, formed blown sand, up behind Broad Have are lovely, especially in late Sprin Well worth a detour. Fp. rou southern end. Freshwater lake formed by damming the valley to th north. On the edge of Stackpo Warren (just east of the Lily Pond) area of blown sand, was a prehistor village; there are round barrows in th shifting sand; flint implements, potte and charred bones have been found.

The Devil's Quoit, a 6ft. pointe stone, is one of three Devil's Quoi which met annually to dance at Sais (Saxon's) Ford and then went bac One is on the Warren, another Stackpole farmyard and the third in field of Sampson Farm.

Villages, Amenities and Short Walks

Bosherston, though a bit busy in th summer, is a most attractive villag with some good houses and cottage Some accommodation, good café an Post Office; pub. The 13th centu church has some good effigies and a interesting 14th century carved cros in the churchyard. No short walks o M.O.D. land, but the Fps. shown te you where one can walk round Bosh erston, and very pleasant it is too.

The Dyfed Archaeological Trust ha published an interesting record of it activities, and an extremely relevar account is given of the excavation o Stackpole Warren.

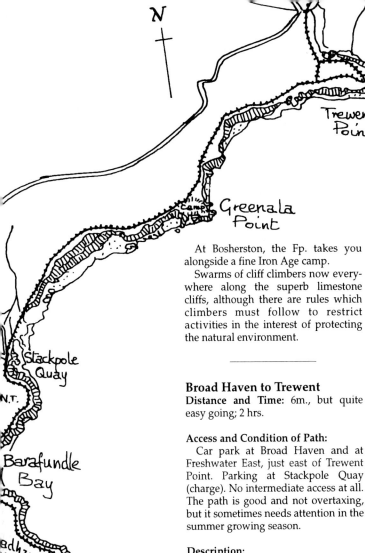

N

Trewent
Point

Greenala
Point

Camp

Stackpole
Quay

N.T.

Barafundle
Bay

edhaven

Stackpole Head

At Bosherston, the Fp. takes you alongside a fine Iron Age camp.

Swarms of cliff climbers now everywhere along the superb limestone cliffs, although there are rules which climbers must follow to restrict activities in the interest of protecting the natural environment.

Broad Haven to Trewent

Distance and Time: 6m., but quite easy going; 2 hrs.

Access and Condition of Path:

Car park at Broad Haven and at Freshwater East, just east of Trewent Point. Parking at Stackpole Quay (charge). No intermediate access at all. The path is good and not overtaxing, but it sometimes needs attention in the summer growing season.

Description:

This is a fine unspoiled stretch of cliff coastline. Barafundle Bay, 2½ miles from Broad Haven, is an excellent sandy beach and not too crowded owing to its relative inaccessibility. It is less than ¾ mile from Stackpole coming from east to

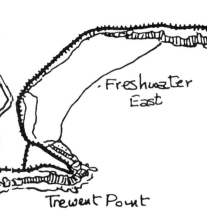

Freshwater East

Trewent Point

west. There are woods on the cliffs and dunes behind the beach. Stackpole Quay, formerly a limestone quarry, is a tiny artificial harbour, now National Trust. Fine square limekiln. Right above Lort's Cave (hole seen from the other side of the bay), south of Barafundle, is a small tumulus, a burial chamber; and at Greenala Point is a fine promontory camp with a number of ramparts. As usual, entrenchments are across the neck of the peninsula, and cliffs protecting the sides. Hut circles within.

Grey, sheer limestones cliffs, flat-topped, to Stackpole cliffs, Beautiful worn red sandstone cliffs, undulating, to Greenala and then Trewent.

Villages, Amenities and Short Walks:
Stackpole Quay has toilets and 'phone. Also N.T. tearooms, though not open all the time in the winter.

Stackpole is a very small, attractive village; P.O., pub, 'phone but nothing else except its church which is dedicated to St Teilo (Elidyr) and has some interesting effigies of the 14th century and the richly decorated tomb of the last of the Norman Stackpoles in the 14th century. The 18th century

mansion, Stackpole Court, w demolished some years ago. T Campbells of Cawdor inherited t estate by marriage (It was the fi Lord Cawdor who led the Cast martin Yeomanry up to Fishguard 1797 and took the surrender of t American Tate after the aborti French Invasion.) But the Cawd have gone back to Scotland and t National Trust has taken over.

The lane from Stackpole bisects t C.P. making a good shortish stretch.

Freshwater East to Manorbier
Distance and Time:
Freshwater East to Manorbier 3½n 1½ hrs.

Access and Condition of Path:
Car parking at Freshwater East ar at Manorbier; the later is a Nation Park car park (small charge Intermediate Fp. access to the Coa Path via both East and West Mo farms, but no right of way for ca any parking must be by permissio only. County road, but very rough.

Description:
Afternoon's walk on good path 1 miles further, is a good beach, agai no vehicular access, so is less popular

Round East Moor cliff, ar Manorbier Bay lies ahead, a pictur book setting for the Castle, church an village. A very popular and crowde

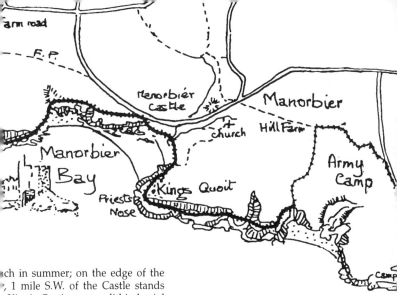

...ch in summer; on the edge of the ..., 1 mile S.W. of the Castle stands ... King's Quoit, a megalithic burial ...mber with a massive 15ft. capstone ...nding on two of its supporters.

...ages, Amenities and Short Walks:
...reshwater East has a café and shop, ...d other amenities.
...oilets at Manorbier beach.
Manorbier is the only village; it has ...ommodation, shops, pubs, Post ...fice but, above all, it has the Castle. ...vately owned and lived in, but open ...visitors from April to October. Of ...th and 13th century construction ...d the walls are well preserved; there ...a fine gateway tower, and a huge ...und tower; inside, a Great Hall and ...ulted chapel. The other interior ...mestic buildings have disappeared ...favour of newer ones. The castle ...s had a remarkably pacific history, ...doubtless it would not be in its ...istine condition today.
...Giraldus Cambrensis (Gerallt ...mro) was born here in 1146. He was ...able Churchman and protagonist of ...e Celtic Church against Canterbury. ...lf Norman and half Welsh, he devoted vain efforts trying to establish the independence of the Welsh church from the clutch of the Normans. Although a friend of Henry II, Richard I and King John, he was never allowed to become Bishop of St David's because he proclaimed widely that the Celtic Church should be independent of Canterbury and made papal visits to push his claim.

He wrote extensively of life in 12th century Wales (and Ireland). In his *Itinerary Through Wales,* Gerald describes Manorbier as 'the most delightful part of Pembroke' with its orchards, fishpond and vineyard. But picturesque as the wild little valley is today, it is unlikely that Gerald would now call it the 'pleasantest spot in Wales' compared with its cultivated state of 800 years ago.

The church too is old, 12th century, at least the nave. Bits have been added: chancel, transepts and battlemented tower.

Manorbier to Penally

Distance and Time:
Manorbier to Army Camp: 1¼m., ½hr.
Army Camp to Lydstep Haven: 2m., ¾ hr.
Lydstep to Penally via Giltar: 3½m., via Fp. from Valleyfield Top: 2½m.

Access and Condition of Path:
Car Parks at Manorbier Beach (charge) Skrinkle Haven and at Lydstep Haven (charge). Elsewhe roadside if feasible.

The condition of the path is good.

Description:
This walk was marred by excrescence of a military camp. It h

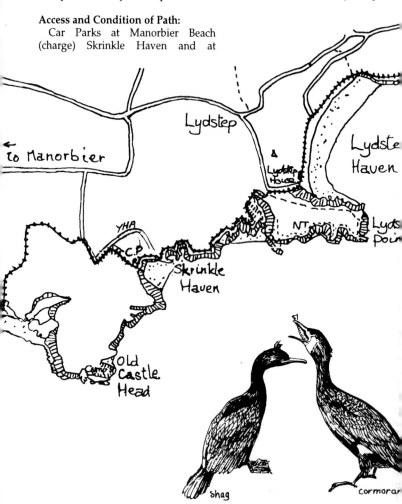

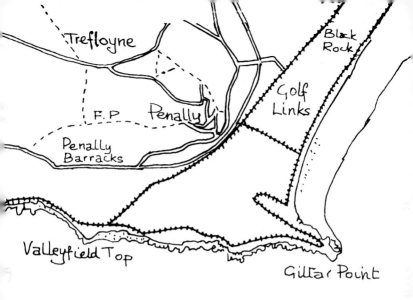

Trefloyne

Black Rock

Golf Links

F. P.

Penally

Penally Barracks

Valleyfield Top

Giltar Point

ow been partly evacuated and the Coast Path taken close to the headand.

The beginning of this walk is shown n the preceding map, so you join this ne on the way from Manorbier to ydstep.

The Palace ruins in Lydstep, somemes said to have been a hunting seat f Bishop Gower of St David's, are a re medieval domestic building; next Post Office and shop: surely worth fficial support to preserve.

Skrinkle Haven and Old Castle Head atter is Out of Bounds), are interting. The latter is a promontory fort, om about 300 B.C. and the former is here the Carboniferous Limestone places the Old Red Sandstone, and astions of rock stick out into the sea.

Beneath and beyond the headland e the famous Lydstep caverns; but ey should be explored at low tide. ne caves and the land above are ational Trust property.

Fulmars and Razorbills nest, and enty of Gulls, Herring mostly, and the ubiquitous Jackdaw. Seals may calve in the autumn in caves along this coast.

A visit to Tenby Museum is advised for anyone interested in prehistoric finds – Old and New Stone Age relics, human and animal, were found in the caves in this area.

There is yet another Army range: a small arms one, on the cliffs. So watch out for red flags which mean keep off.

Villages, Amenities and Short Walks:

Penally, itself a small village, was once of greater fame than Tenby for it was the centre of the missionary endeavour of St Teilo, a Penally man, and the great ecclesiastical rival of St David. Visit the Churchyard for the famous Celtic Cross.

Fp. up from coast to road via Hill Farm. Fp. right round Lydstep Headland – half hour walk (National Trust) and Fp. down to each end of and across Lydstep Haven, which is private above high water. Cart track down south end.

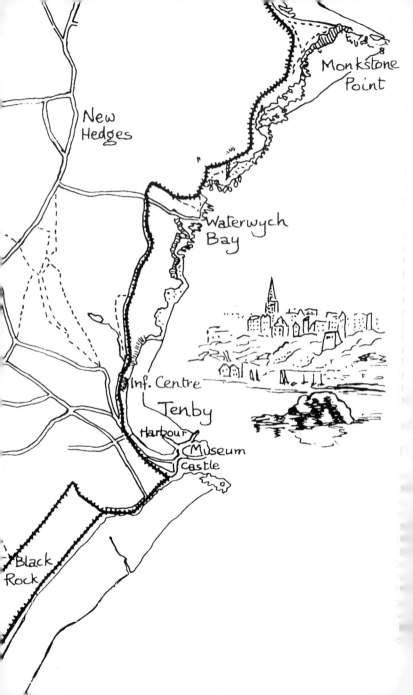

New Hedges

Monkstone Point

Waterwych Bay

Inf. Centre

Tenby

Harbour

Museum

Castle

Black Rock

Giltar Point (or Penally)
– Tenby - Monkstone Point

Distance and Time:
Giltar Point to Tenby Information Centre: 2m., 1hr. Tenby Information Centre to Monkstone 2¼m., 1 hr.

Access and Condition of Path:

There is in fact no official Coast Path through Tenby and parking is chancy: in the summer everywhere is crowded. There is a car park in Penally, and several in Tenby but you will have to take your chance. There is no parking at the Monkstone end of this walk, not, in fact, until you come to Saundersfoot on the next map. Either start from Giltar or Penally, go along the beach to the Esplanade, go up through Tenby, keeping to the seaward side of the town, up to the Norton, where the Information Centre is, and then out to North Cliff where the Coast Path starts. Or along to Black Pool either from Penally or Giltar and then, past the railway bridge, follow the line to the station, and up through the town.

There is a Fp. access to Monkstone from the main road via Trevayne Farm.

Description:

This is an interesting but hardly scenic walk. The sands are fine and the town interesting historically; in the off season it is extremely attractive architecturally; in the summer it is so thronged that one can hardly see anything. The start of the Coast Path is on the old Waterwynch Lane, a pleasant shady bridleway, off the coast, but you may well see a fox there. At the top of the hill on the seaward side is a stile giving access to Allen's View, a wonderful viewing spot. The Coast Path skirts Waterwynch (though the beach is down on the right) and the path leads to the coast, where it stays up to Monkstone. It can be muddy round Waterwynch in wet weather. A good, exposed cliff walk later, not too well marked at a couple of places in the past at times, and there were a couple of surprisingly strenuous stretches, but in general it is fine for all walkers.

Town and Amenities:

Tenby (W: Dinbych y Pysgod) after a chequered history, became a fashionable watering place in Georgian times.

It has very reasonably been called the Brighton of West Wales. It is indeed very unlike the rest of the county, traditional rail connections with England and South Wales and well organised tourism produced crowds even before the days of cars, that should have warned those responsible for including this whole area in the National Park.

Tenby has everything to make a seaside town jolly (except parking space). A small traditionally crowded museum in a fine position: on the headland, in the ruins of the 13th century castle, close to the statue of Prince Albert. Good 13th century town walls – or what is left of them.

There are a lot of hotels and guest houses – some architecurally handsome, others purely functional. There is an interesting National Trust property, the Tudor Merchants' House from about 1500, to visit; and a distinguished 15th century church. And excellent beaches. St Catherine's Fort, late Victorian, was an extension of the Milford Haven defence system.

A pleasant town to wander in, so an hour or two off from the Coast Path is worthwhile. In fact, when you do re-start the Coast Path, it is surprising how isolated the walking can become past Waterwynch.

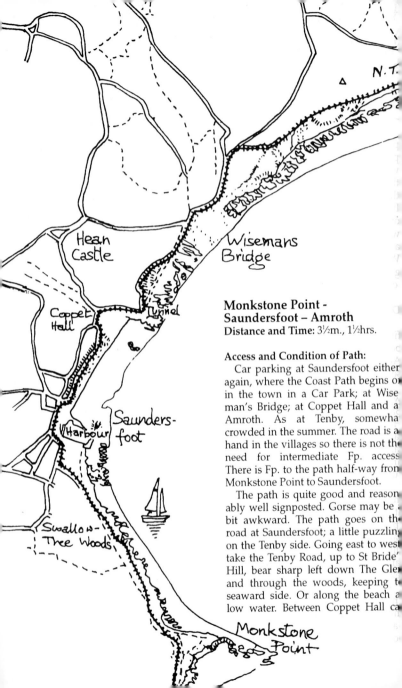

N.T.

Hean Castle

Wisemans Bridge

Coppet Hall

Tunnel

Saunders-foot

Harbour

Swallow-Tree Woods

Monkstone Point

Monkstone Point - Saundersfoot – Amroth
Distance and Time: 3½m., 1½hrs.

Access and Condition of Path:

Car parking at Saundersfoot either again, where the Coast Path begins or in the town in a Car Park; at Wiseman's Bridge; at Coppet Hall and at Amroth. As at Tenby, somewhat crowded in the summer. The road is at hand in the villages so there is not the need for intermediate Fp. access. There is Fp. to the path half-way from Monkstone Point to Saundersfoot.

The path is quite good and reasonably well signposted. Gorse may be a bit awkward. The path goes on the road at Saundersfoot; a little puzzling on the Tenby side. Going east to west take the Tenby Road, up to St Bride's Hill, bear sharp left down The Glen and through the woods, keeping to seaward side. Or along the beach at low water. Between Coppet Hall ca

ark and Wiseman's Bridge the Coast
ath now goes up through the
oodland on top of the cliff because
e cliffs are crumbling. In fact, even
is path is being slowly moved inland.
one wants to risk the bottom path
e can have a very interesting round
alk through woods one way then
ong the old tramway back. At
'iseman's Bridge, going west to east,
o up the road, bear right and the path
ins it.

escription:
This is an artificially broken walk, to
t in with the map. In practice, it is
etter to start from Tenby. Tenby to
mroth is a good half-day's walk with
ome hard going.
This is fine stretch, not remote, but
ith splendid views over Carmarthen
ay to the Gower Peninsula, Worms
lead. It is rough cliff, but with wood-
nd too, and interspersed with vil-
ges, so the amenities are there. There
re a few strenuous places and some
urprisingly steep.
As at other points round the coast,
e woodland, mostly scrub oak here
t Swallowtree, indicates a sheltered
ot. Don't miss, when you come into
aundersfoot, the cliffs; the sharp anti-
inal fold in the Coal Measures is
amous, and features in many geology
xt-books.
Coal mining of high quality
nthracite was important here from
he 16th century until 1930.
aundersfoot became the export
oint; and the tunnel you go through
at Coppet Hall was a colliery tramway.
Amroth beach is famous for its
'drowned forest', some 7,000 years
old. At very low water, tree stumps
can be seen; fossilised nuts, antlers,
animal bone and Neolithic flints have
been found.
The N.T. own the coast land between
Amroth and Wiseman's Bridge and
inland, including the fine Colby
Woodland Garden.

Villages & Amenities
Saundersfoot is a recent village. It
didn't exist in the 18th century. The
harbour is early Victorian and was
built for coal export; ships were even
built here. Now it is a holiday resort
pure and simple, the harbour filled
with small boats.
Wiseman's Bridge had its moment
of glory in 1943 when Sir Winston
Churchill, who stayed at the Wiseman's Bridge Inn, watched a rehearsal
of the Normandy landings when
Saundersfoot to Pendine was
swarming with landing-craft, soldiers
and guns.
Amroth is a small pleasant hamlet
with a lovely beach.
The whole area of Saundersfoot,
Wiseman's Bridge and Amroth is one
long stretch devoted to tourism. It is
basically modern. Whereas there was
an ancient Tenby whose narrow streets
betoken a medieval past with genuine
town walls and Five Arches to clog up
the traffic, the 'newer' villages to the
east are choked by sheer weight of
cars.
The eastern end of Amroth is the
Carmathenshire boundary and the
end of the path.

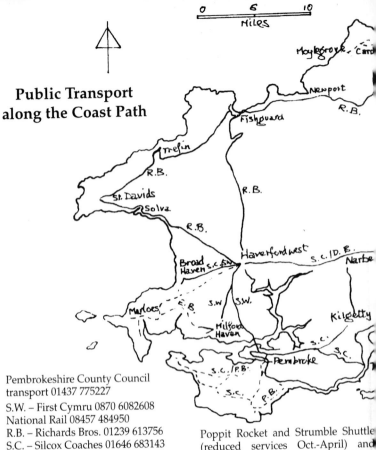

Public Transport along the Coast Path

Pembrokeshire County Council
transport 01437 775227

S.W. – First Cymru 0870 6082608
National Rail 08457 484950
R.B. – Richards Bros. 01239 613756
S.C. – Silcox Coaches 01646 683143
E.B. – Edwards Bros. 01437 890230

The above map indicates the bus routes along the coast. The solid line is regular services, the dotted line occasional. There is also a railway line along the south coast and to Milford & Fishguard. These routes are covered by a variety of companies listed here with their main phone number. Tourist Information Centres and the Council (phone number above) will have information.

The Council are now also providing various minibus services such as the Poppit Rocket and Strumble Shuttle (reduced services Oct.-April) and Puffin Shuttle (summer only).

The Poppit Rocket goes from Poppit, through Moylegrove, Newport Sands, Dinas and Pwllgwaelod to Fishguard.

The Strumble Shuttle goes from Fishguard, through Strumble Head Trefasser, Tregwynt, Mathry, Abercastle, Trefin and Porthgain to St Davids.

The Puffin Shuttle goes from St Davids to Milford Haven along the coast.

The routes are not marked on the map.